Some Pioneers And Pilgrims On The Prairies Of Dakota

by

John B. Reese And H.B. Reese

Double9 BOOKS

Some Pioneers And Pilgrims On The Prairies Of Dakota

by John B. Reese And H.B. Reese

ISBN: 978-93-59958-80-4

Published by

DOUBLE 9 BOOKS
2/13-B, Ansari Road
Daryaganj, New Delhi – 110002
info@double9books.com
www.double9books.com
Tel. 011-40042856

ABOUT THE AUTHOR

"Some Pioneers and Pilgrims at the Prairies of Dakota" stands as a testomony to the literary prowess of authors John B. Reese and H. B. Reese. This collaborative masterpiece is renowned for its charming exploration of ancient evaluation, forging connections between readers and the wealthy tapestry of the past. John B. Reese, a great writer, invested exquisite effort in crafting this work, bridging the gap among history and the human enjoy. Through his writing, he aspired to facilitate expertise and empathy among readers, fostering a feel of shared background and commonplace humanity. The brilliance of John B. Reese and H. B. Reese shines through of their writing, which is a fusion of creativity and ardour. Their narratives delivery readers to diverse landscapes and evoke a spectrum of emotions, developing an immersive and unforgettable studying enjoy. The beauty and simplicity of their prose make certain that their extraordinary memories are handy and exciting to a huge audience, further improving the effect of their literary legacy. In "Some Pioneers and Pilgrims on the Prairies of Dakota," John B. Reese and H. B. Reese have left an indelible mark on the arena of historic literature, inviting readers to embark on an adventure thru time and reminiscence, fostering a deeper reference to our shared human records.

CONTENTS

Chapter I
Prying Open the Door into the Rich Lands of the Dakotas

Previous to April, 1858, Dakota Territory for a century or more had been the hunting ground and undisputed possession of the Yankton Sioux. However, for some years before this date many adventurous, enterprising members of the white race in the adjoining states of Iowa, Minnesota and Nebraska, had cast covetous eyes across the borders. Not a few even followed their eyes and entered in spite of the prohibition of the government and the hostilities of the Indian. Many more, encamped along the borders were watching the negotiations between the government and the Yanktons, eager and alert to step over the line the very instant the door should be opened.

According to the available data on the Indian history of this region, previous to 1750 it was occupied by the Omahas, who held the Big Sioux and James river valleys. These were driven out about 1750 by the Teton Sioux, who came previously from the woods of Minnesota. The Teton Sioux also engaged the Rees, then having strongholds on the Missouri, especially in and around Pierre, and after a forty years' struggle drove them north to Grand River and then to where their remnants are still found in the vicinity of Fort Berthold, North Dakota.

At this time of the Treaty, this region was held by the Yankton and Yanktonais Sioux, who had been driven from western Iowa by the Ottos about 1780 and had settled the lower James River Valley.

The first attempt at a settlement at Yankton was made in the spring of 1858 by one W.P. Holman, his son C.J. Holman, both of Sergeants Bluff, Iowa, and Ben Stafford, together with four or five others from Sioux City. In anticipation of an early treaty these men came up on the Nebraska side of the river and, crossing over at Yankton, built a camp. But about a month later the Indians, jealous of their hunting grounds and suspicious of the designs of the intruders, drove them back across the river.

The next May, however, on the strength of a false rumor that the treaty had been ratified, these men floated logs across from their Nebraska camp, working all night, and next day laid twelve foundations. The following day construction of the first log cabin was begun. But before this could be finished some seventy-five Indians appeared and began to hurl the newly founded city of Yankton into the river. It was fortunate, as Mr. Holman, who was one of the party, suggests, that the new settlers had left their guns on the other side. For had they had their arms they would hardly have been able to submit to the destruction of their town without a fight, and if it had come to a fight the Indians were as yet too many. As it was, the intruders resorted to diplomacy, and by much "fine talk" succeeded in saving most of their belongings as well as of the construction and in holding their ground. The next day a feast was promptly made to Chief Dog's Claw and his warriors, and as is always the case with men, red or white, this feast had the desired effect, at least for the time being. The log house was built altho subsequently burned in October, 1858.

The first permanent buildings, as far as we can ascertain, were those of the Frost, Todd Co. Trading Post. There were, of course, Indian tepees scattered over the present city and vicinity of Yankton, but these appeared and disappeared again with the movements of their inhabitants. There was also about this time a cabin built on the east side of the present James River bridge by J.M. Stone, who operated a ferry boat.

It is stated by the late Mayor J.R. Hanson of Yankton, who came to Yankton with a party of pioneers from Winona, Minnesota, in 1858, that more than one hundred locations of 160 acres had already been staked out in the vicinity of Yankton on his arrival. These, of course, later had to be filed on in the regular way when the land became legally opened to settlers.

As already indicated, the treaty for the opening of this land for settlement was at last arranged in 1858, but it was not until July 10, 1859, that the land was legally opened for settlers by ratification of the treaty. On that very date the streams of expectant immigrants, waiting on the borders of Nebraska and Iowa, poured in like a flood and the towns of Vermilion, Meckling, Yankton and Bon Homme were all founded in a day. On the 22nd of July Elk Point was first settled.

An interesting story is told of the long extended Indian pow-wows and the fiery harangues on the part of the chiefs before they finally relinquished their ancient camping ground and the graves of their fathers on the present site of Yankton. The government had made tempting offers in the way of regular rations of food, blankets and many other commodities, not to speak of money and large reservations of land to be guaranteed for the exclusive possession of the tribe. These immediate benefits and creature comforts made a powerful appeal to the common crowd among the Indians.

This faction was led by Chief Struck by the Ree, who was friendly to the Whites. The other chiefs, however, many of whom were shrewd and able men and thought with their heads rather than, as the crowd did, with their stomachs, keenly realized what the little act of signing this treaty involved. They saw that it meant that when they should fold their tepees and journey westward this time they could never return. They knew that it meant the final abandonment of their immemorial hunting grounds and the beautiful camping site of Yankton with the graves of their fathers, to the pale faces who would come in like a flood and once in they could no more be turned back than the tides of the sea. In many and prolonged councils these chiefs, such as Smutty Bear and Mad Bull, had pressed upon their people these and other considerations against the signing of the White man's treacherous papers. With burning words of appeal, now to this motive now to that, with stinging rebuke of those who would so lightly sell out their birthright and ancestral heritage, as well as that of their children and the unborn generations to come, they spoke with an eloquence which seemed for the time to stir and elevate even the craven spirits of those who had favored the treaty. But just at this point, when it looked as tho the treaty would be rejected and the Indians would stay where they were, a government boat carrying large supplies of food and other desirable commodities whistled down the river. The word was soon passed that these treasures would be taken up the river some thirty miles to their new home near the present site of Springfield, and be distributed to the Indians in case they would now vacate and carry out the treaty. The temptation was too great. All the oratory was forgotten in the prospect of food, clothing and glittering spangles. There was no more argument. The tepees with strange and significant rapidity and universality began to come down and get loaded. The travaux, loaded with the whole household belongings and also in some cases with children, began to move silently but surely toward the West, heading for the rendezvous appointed by the steam boat people. Deserted by their people, the chiefs, realizing that they were face to face with an irresistible tide and were fighting a hopeless fight, followed their people with sad and bitter spirits as they all trekked toward the setting sun, never more to return to the rich valley and far-flung prairies of the lower Missouri. Before the vanquished and vanishing Indian had gotten out of sight over the hills the eager White man was moving in.

Chapter II
The Second Coming of the Norsemen to America

It is now quite generally conceded that Leif Erikson and his party, as also other adventurous spirits of Iceland and Norway, visited these shores half a thousand years before Columbus. The second coming of the Norsemen, or the immigration to America from Norway in any considerable numbers, began about 1840. Illinois, Wisconsin, Iowa, Minnesota, Nebraska, and the Dakotas, about in the order named, came to receive this large influx of the hardy Norsemen. Wherever they went they took their full share, and more, of helping to build the railroads, fell the forests, subdue the prairies and build a Christian civilization.

The first settlement of considerable size in South Dakota was, as far as we can learn, made in 1860, between the James river and Gayville. Other settlers followed in the succeeding years, spreading out over the bottom and later up on the prairie to the north. Among those who came to the vicinity of Yankton in the decade of 1860-70 we would mention the following: Ole Odland, '62; Ole C. Pederson, '66; Lars Hanson, '66; O.L. Hanson, '67; Ole Pederson, '67; Nec. Hanson, '68; Lars Bergsvenson, '68; Andrew Simonson, '68; J.M. Johnson (Irene),'68; Ole Bjerke, '69; Ole Lien (Volin), formerly of Brule, Union County, '68, with his sons Charles and Edward Lien; Jorgen Bruget; Christian Marendahl, '67; Nels Brekke, '67; Peder Engen; Gunder Olson, '68; Haldo Saether, '69; Sivert Nysether also came about this time.

Iver Bjerke and Mark Johnson appear to be the first native born children of the Scandinavian immigrants in this part of the country, both being born in '69. However, Ole Jelley of Clay County holds the honor of being, not only the first child born of Norse parents in the state, but of being, as far as is known, the first male white child born in South Dakota. He was born March 2, 1860.

Others who came in this period were Ole Skaane, '69; C. Freng, '69; J.T. Nedved, '68; G. Gulbranson, '69; P.J. Freng, '69; Halvor Aune, '69.

In the next decade, 1870-80, we find these well known names: I.S. Fagerhaug (Irene), '70; O. Kjelseth and two sons, George and C.J. Kjelseth, '70; Ole Lee (Aune), '70; O.P. Olsen, '70; A.O. Saugstad, '70; O.J. Anderson (Irene), '70; H. Hoxeng with his sons Thore and Jens, '70; P.J. Nyberg, '72; J.J. Nissen, '72; John Aaseth, '72; Peter Carlson, '72; the Bagstad brothers, Iver, Mathias and Emil; and Hans Helgerson, '74; John Gjevik and Lars Aaen, '75.

The settlement in Clay Creek was begun a little earlier than Turkey Creek, or about '69. Among those who first broke the virgin sod there were O. Skaane, O. Gustad, H. Hagen, and his son Albert, the latter also sharing the honor with B.B. Haugan of breaking the first furrow of the sod in Mayfield Township. Then there were Benjamin Anderson, Peter Olaus, R. Olsen, A.O. Saugstad and Fredrik Aune.

It was at the beginning of this decade, 1870-80, that the settlement of the Turkey Creek Valley was begun by I. Fagerhaug, S. Hinseth, Halvor Hinseth (1870); and Ole Solem; Jens Eggen to the south, and John Rye to the north end of the valley.

We are aware that this list of early settlers is far from complete. No complete list could be made at this time, as many of them are long since gone and forgotten. We hope, however, that this is fairly comprehensive, and should we meet with enough favor to warrant another edition of this memorial, then, by the help of some of our readers, we may be able to gather up some of the missing names which ought to be included. In such an edition there should also be a record of the children, boys and girls, of these first settlers. This would be of more interest and value in the years to come, as a matter of reference, than we can now realize. To be able to prove by the records that we came from one of the "old families" of first settlers may be an object a hundred years from now.

On the adventures, hardships, struggles and triumphs of these first Norse settlers on the Missouri bottom we cannot dwell, nor do we have much available material, as there are not many left now to tell the story. There were Indians as in the Massacre of '62, when Judge Amiden and his son were killed near Sioux Falls. There were fires, droughts and blizzards. Then grasshoppers in '63, '64, '74, '76. And all the time the lack of even what are now the common necessities, not to speak of the comforts and conveniences of life. The table had to be provided largely from what the settlers themselves could produce from the untamed soil and the clothes from the coarse cheap cloth available at the few towns, such as blue denim for men and calico for women.

The settlers in this region had one advantage in their start on a bare soil. Wood for fuel and timber was available. While this timber was largely cottonwood and willow, yet out of the cottonwood, and occasionally oak, they were able to construct log houses. This was quite an advantage here, as dugouts on this level and low lying land would not have been even as satisfactory as on the prairie.

These men and women who led in subduing the raw, untamed soil may be likened to soldiers in the first line trenches as also to shock troops. In order that others might reap the fruits of victory some had to be sacrificed. Many of these front liners perished early in the struggle. Others have come down even to the present. But within and outside they bear the marks, D.S.C's, may I say, of the great days of battle.

Chapter III
The First Settlement of the Prairie From the Missouri Bottom North as Far as the Turkey Creek Valley

Among the first to homestead and build on this tract, in early days called the South Prairie, were, as far as we can learn, Christian Marendahl; Nils Brekke, '67; John Sleeper, '68; Gunder Olsen, '68; Peder Engen, Sivert Nysether, Esten Nyhus, Ole Liabo, Iver Furuness, and Miss Marie Hoxeng came during '68-'69. Ole Bjerke and H. Sether came in '69. About this time came also Lars Aaen. The Hoxengs came the next year, or 1870, and Hans Dahl and Lars Eide a little later.

It may be of interest as illustrating how these people got on their chosen locations, to describe in brief the experiences of some of them.

Ole Bjerke came to Sioux City in the spring of '69. This little village was then the "farthest west" as far as the railroad was concerned. Thru an acquaintance of his, Joe Sleeper, I believe, he had become interested in the far away prairie north of Yankton, which was open for settlement. Accordingly he bought, thru Mr. Halseth of Sioux City, a yoke of oxen and a wagon, the standard equipment of the pioneer settler of those days. These oxen, like most of their tribe, were wild and unruly; ran away, broke the wagon to pieces and were lost for some weeks. Finally the trip was made over the winding prairie trail westward thru Brule and Vermilion, thence along the bluffs to their destination. It was a long, weary trip thru the tall grass, and the accommodations in the way of food and sleep at the few human habitations along the way were not of the kind to cheer the weary pilgrims. For in most cases a rude shelter was all they could obtain, having to provide food and bedding for themselves, the owners often being bachelors, sometimes "at home" and often not at home for months.

On arriving at their destination, Mr. and Mrs. Bjerke were able to share shelter with a kind neighbor already on the ground until they could construct one of their own. Here, soon after their arrival, Iver Bjerke was born and was the first child to receive baptism in this settlement. In this hospitable home of Mr. and Mrs. Bjerke were also held the first religious services in this vicinity, in 1869. These services were conducted by Rev. Nesse from Brule, who became the first pastor of these people. There was at this time, '69, no neighbor to the north nearer than Swan Lake, eighteen miles away.

Chapter IV
First Settlement and Settlers of the "South Prairie," 1861-71, Memorable Trip in Search of Work

However, in '69 and '70 there came to be a considerable settlement on the South Prairie of the people already named and others who came in the latter '60's and early 70's.

When we say that people "settled" here at this time it must not be interpreted to mean that they began to put up good buildings, break the sod and raise grain and cattle. These activities were for many as yet years away. As a general thing a rude dwelling of logs, sod, or a dugout was made to shelter the family and to fulfil the law in regard to getting deed to the land. Also a few acres were broken, perhaps five or ten, to comply with these homestead requirements. Then about the next thing was for the men folks to strike out for the forts on the upper Missouri in order to earn a little money, by cutting wood or working on other government jobs, to support themselves and their families. This work and the wretched food and "accommodations" given them would have broken these men in body and spirit had they not been young and vigorous in body as well as unconquerable in spirit.

Perhaps we can reproduce the experiences of many of the above named homesteaders of the '60's and early '70's by giving the actual story of one group who went up the river to find work, as related to us by one of the parties, Ole Lee, now living near Volin.

Mr. Lee came to America in 1870, May 18th, and landed, like most of the above named, in Sioux City, where his brother Halvor Aune had already preceded him. With only 35 cents with which to start in the new country, Mr. Lee counted himself fortunate in finding a job at $1.75 per day, even tho board had to be paid out of this. But even this fortune did not last long, for Sioux City was a small place and had little development at that time. Yet, however short Ole was in cash, he did have some capital which could be invested in the new country and would in time compel success. He had a good, sound body, great courage, a cheerful disposition and a good talking apparatus, altho as yet operating mostly in the Norwegian language. So having learned that there was work and better pay than he had been getting, in connection with the steamboat traffic and the government forts on the upper Missouri, he in company with a number of others started west to seek fortune as also adventure. As most of these men were young and unmarried, the Viking spirit of adventure and daring was not absent.

It was in the spring of 1871 that these young men, gathered at Yankton, decided to trek over the country to Fort Sully, 300 miles away, in search of work.

They had among them scarcely any money and some even owed their winter's board. So at first they thought of starting out afoot. But thru an acquaintance of one of the party they were able to buy an ox team on time, agreeing to pay $180.00 for the same, including an old wagon. They were able to buy a few provisions, such as flour and salt pork, for their own use on the way, and some sacks of oats for the oxen as hay or grass could not be depended on, the vast prairie often being burned off.

There were eighteen of these young explorers in all and while one drove the oxen by turns the other seventeen walked behind the wagon. Besides the two brothers already mentioned, there were in this company Emret and Sivert Mjoen; also Sivert and Christopher Haakker, Ingibricht Satrum, Iver Furuness, Ole Solem, Ole Yelle, Albert Meslo, Anders Krengness and Thomas Berg. I have not the names of the others of the party.

These young men, altho afoot and with meager provisions, on their way toward a far-off destination and unknown conditions, yet trudged along day after day with jokes and laughter. At noon or night, wherever they happened to be on the broad plains, the same cooking routine was performed, each taking his turn. Get out the long handled frying pan, the fire having been built, fry pancakes or flap-jacks, and perhaps a little pork, and boil some coffee. Then if it was the evening meal they would sit around the fire a while to stretch their weary legs, smoke a pipe, talk over and speculate on the prospects ahead and then roll up in their blankets for the night.

One day, as they were nearing Fort Thompson, having followed the course of the river so far, they met a man driving a mule team. Surmising from their appearance that these men were in a situation to accept work of most any kind or on any condition, he stopped to parley with them. He had a government contract to cut 900 cords of wood on an island below Ft. Thompson. So he offered these men $2 per cord to cut this wood. They were only too eager to grasp this first opportunity, especially as he was to furnish them board. But what should they do with their joint property—oxen and wagon? The man, realizing he had made a "find" in these eager strong handed men, didn't let this stand in the way but bought the outfit for $185.00. They thus made $5.00 on the deal, and in regular democratic style it was voted in assembly to send back the $180.00 due the former owner of the oxen; sell the remainder of the oats and with the total proceeds have a little "refreshment" before they began their summer's work. This they did in reaching the fort, and the only refreshments to be had in those places being in liquid form, there was just enough money in the treasury to buy them "one each."

Now, let it be remembered by this and all coming generations that this was the first commercial co-operative enterprise, as far as we know, in this part of the country, and that it yielded a profit—it "liquidated."

They now immediately began cutting wood on this island below Fort Thompson, and it was well that they had had some "refreshment," for what they now received in the way of board was fearfully and wonderfully made. It consisted of spoiled pork and wormy flour, rejected by the soldier commissary at the fort and bought for little or nothing by this shameless contractor to feed these unsuspecting men. Out of this material, a not over clean negro cook made two standard dishes—soda biscuits and fried pork. Often the remnants of the worms, embalmed and baked into the biscuits could be plainly seen.

The men bore as patiently as they could with this sickening food, for there was little else to do now under their circumstances. But their stomachs rebelled, however, and the men became so weakened thru continued diarrhea that they could scarcely lift the ax at times. Yet with characteristic Viking spirit they "stuck it out" until the 900 cords were hewn. The men now separated, some going back to Yankton or vicinity. Ole Lee and his brother Halvor, however, pushed on up to Fort Sully, or Cheyenne Agency, where the former remained for five years without seeing civilization again in the meantime. By this time Mr. Lee, as well as others of the above named company, had been able to save up a little money and homesteaded in Yankton county, where some of them and many of their descendants live to this day, not a few of them being worth $100,000 each. You recall we began our narrative of one of them with a capital of 35 cents. The explanation of this, of 35 cents to $100,000; of the borrowed ox team and rickety wagon to the finest automobiles in the market; of the sod shanty or dugout to the big modern houses with all the latest conveniences which some of these men have today, lies in two or three words—America and the Norse immigrants' great characteristics, industrially speaking—industry and thrift.

We have suggested the striking change which fifty years have wrought in the outward circumstances of these men. Would that the intervening years could have been equally kind to the men themselves as to their earthly tabernacles! But such could not be the case, altho several of them are still living and a number spending their declining years as neighbors in the vicinity of Volin. The heat and toil of many summers have wrinkled their brows; the snows of many winters and some sorrows and cares have whitened the hair and given a stoop to the shoulders. The step is a little less firm now than when they together marched over the prairie to the west; their laughter has lost some of its ring, and yet it is there. With their children and grandchildren they are enjoying a little deserved rest before the final journey to the last sunset of life's trail.

There is Ole Lee, Ole Solem, Halvor Hinseth and the Hoxengs, still active and living in good, comfortable homes and in the same neighborhood. There is Ole Bjerke, once tall and straight as a young pine of the forest, now a little bent over and gray. There, too, is his wife, remarkably well preserved in both body and mental faculties. How many generations of "newcomers" have received a hearty welcome and hospitality in these homes and have been by them helped to get a start in the new land! Long will they live enshrined in the hearts and memories of the many who have enjoyed the hospitality of their firesides.

Yes, most of these pioneers of forty to sixty years ago have already struck the long trail and gone to that "West" which is the farthest and the final. Of the few who remain, the earthly tabernacles are leaning more and more toward the earth from which they came, and in a very short time not one will be left standing. Yet because man's immortal hope burns strongly in many of them, the building of flesh, tho feebler than of yore, is glorious with that light which the years and the eternities cannot dim nor extinguish, for it is eternal in the Heavens.

Chapter V
The Settlements on Turkey Creek, and Clay Creek, '70-71

The settlement in Turkey Creek was made in 1870. A man by the name of John Hovde, who had homesteaded in Union county some years previously, made a trip back to Norway and on his return the following people came over with him: Anfin Utheim and wife; Olaf Stolen; Haakon Hoxeng with his two sons, already referred to, and one daughter; Stingrim Hinseth with wife and one baby daughter, Mary; Halvor Hinseth; Ingebright Fagerhaug; and Marit Nysether, who later became his wife, and a number of other men and women who went to other parts of the country.

These people reached Sioux City May 18, 1870. There some of the men of the company found work on the railroad. The others, including S. and H. Hinseth and Miss Nysether, journeyed on by ox team toward their friends already described as settled on the South Prairie, i.e., north of the present Volin. Their baggage went by steam boat to Yankton. Mr. and Mrs. S. Hinseth, who had a little six-year-old baby daughter, went by stage as far as Vermilion and there transferred to the ox team, the stage going on to Yankton.

We will here quote from a brief narrative which Mr. S. Hinseth, at our request, prepared for this record just before his death (1918). As Mr. Hinseth was one of the outstanding leaders in this immigration movement and in the building up of the new country, both materially and spiritually, we are very fortunate in getting these memoranda directly from him. We regret that he was cut off before he could finish them.

"We reached our destination in Yankton county on a Sunday. That day there was church service at the home of Mr. and Mrs. O. Bjerke, conducted by pastor Nesse of Brule, Union county.

"There was no possibility of getting work in the neighborhood, so a number of us went up to Fort Randall, where we obtained work cutting cord wood for steamboat use. We remained there until fall, when Halvor

Stables were made from a little frame work of rails, for roof at least, and this was covered with hay or straw. The walls were usually the same materials and were eaten up during the winter as a general occurrence and had to be restored in the fall.

We have heard Halvor Hinseth and other pioneers in these settlements tell of their experiences in going to mill in the first ten years or more. As the grasshoppers destroyed most of the small grain in '74 and '76 the settlers had barely enough for flour and a little seed. The nearest mill was three miles south of St. Helena, Nebraska. As this was south of the present Gayville they would either have to go by Yankton to cross the river or else cross on the ice in the winter. Mr. H. Hinseth relates one trip, vivid in his memory, when they with their loads got into deep snow out on the bottom; got lost in the brush south of Gayville; were refused shelter when they at last found a light from a cabin in the brush; how their horses gave out and the sleds broke down and the men themselves were about used up. Sometimes they would be overtaken by a snowstorm on their trip and be snowed in for several days, so these mill trips would often take a week's time and more toil and hardship than we can describe. But they managed to get back sometime and with flour for the family.

Chapter VI
The Great Immigration of 1880—Cause of

If a man had stood by the king's highway leading from Opdal, Norway, to the seaport town of Trondhjem, in the month of April, 1880, he could have witnessed a strange and significant scene. Here comes a procession of twenty or more sleds, each drawn by a single small horse. The sleds were heavily loaded with large, blue-tinted chests, as also trunks, satchels and numerous smaller articles of household and family use. Riding on top of these loads are mothers with little children as also a number of grandmothers, the latter upwards of seventy years of age. A number of lighter sleds, or cutters, are also in the procession. These belong to friends of this pilgrim procession, who are accompanying them part way and are now about to say, or have already said, their final farewell and Godspeed to these pilgrims—their friends and relations. This may explain in part the fact that the men walk by the side of their loads in silence, with downcast eyes and a lump in their throats, while the women show clear traces of recent tears. Nor can we blame them for succumbing for the moment to their emotions when we come to understand the meaning of this strange scene.

These people, about sixty in number, this day were leaving that spot on God's earth most dear to them; leaving the birthplace and the resting-place of a hundred generations of their ancestors, they were looking for the last time on their former homes and on the dear familiar spots so well known from their childhood. They had just looked for the last time upon the faces of their friends and near relatives and spoken the last words, and soon they were to see the receding outlines of the mountain peaks of their beloved fatherland, nevermore to see them again. For they were on the way to America, and America was very far off in those days, and to most people going there the way back was forever closed. So to these people these last glimpses and handshakes and words were the final, as far as this world went, and they were all too well aware of it.

But let us pause in the journey at this point, while still under the influence of the nearby majestic mountains, robed in evergreen and crowned with the snows of generations, so as to get acquainted with the individuals of this company and also to learn the causes which could lead these people to an undertaking so fraught with momentous destiny for all of them and for their descendants to the end of time. As we have already surmised, these people were not light-minded adventurers or people who had nothing to risk or lose. On the contrary, they were deeply rooted where they were and they did not pluck up their life by the roots to be transplanted in a far-off, unknown soil without careful consideration and a great motive.

First we meet Berhaug Rise (later written Reese) who seems to be a leader in this particular group we have before us. He is a man of about forty-five, of spare build and medium height. He has a family consisting of wife and five children—four boys and one girl; also his mother who is nearly seventy years of age. The children's names were Ole, eleven years; Halvor, nine; John, coming seven; Sivert, five; and Mary, three years, and named after the grandmother.

Next we get acquainted with Halvor Hevle, a man also of about forty-five, but because of a terrible affliction of rheumatism, was bent over so that his face is toward the ground. He is accompanied by his wife, Marit, but they have no children.

Then there is Thore Fossem with his wife, his mother and one little girl, Marie, named after the grandmother. It should be explained here that while this last named family was not present in the above group just at this point of the story but came a little later, yet because Mr. Fossem belongs by every other circumstance to this group, and in spiritual kinship and motive particularly with the above two, we include him here. With Thore Fossem came Ingebricht Satrum with one of his boys, I believe, but most of his family came over a year or two later.

The above three men had all been owners of small or medium sized farms and had advanced money for transportation to most of the others in the party from the recent sale of their properties. The remainder of the party, as we shall see, was largely composed of middle aged tradesmen, young unattached men and girls, practically all of them without means of their own to make the long journey. Most of these middle aged men of trades had left large families behind and expected to earn enough money in the new land to repay their own passage and also to send for their families as soon as possible. But more of this later, for the when and the how of the repayment of some of these transportations would be out of place here, tho not without some very interesting features.

One of these men who was master of a trade and who also belongs, in the sense of an absolutely kindred spirit, to the above three, was Iver Sneve. He left wife and five children, taking with him his two older boys, Ingebricht and Ole.

In much the same economic relation was Anders Ellingson Loe, a shoemaker by trade. Also Arne Loe, who was a mason and left wife and three children behind until he could send for them.

To this class should also be added Ingebricht Brenden, having left his wife and five children—Ingebricht, Knut, Elli, Sigrid and Kjerstine.

Among the younger married men were John Lien with wife and one boy, Esten, as also his mother, who was another member of the considerable group of grandmas in the party.

Here should be mentioned also Lars Hansen Almen with wife and two boys—Hans and Olaus as also Mrs. Almen's mother, who makes the fourth member of the remarkable grandmother class in this group of pilgrims to a faraway country.

Then there were the following young and middle aged unmarried men and women: Ildri Loe, now Mrs. Sneve of Inwood, Iowa; Kari Rathe; Marit Myren; Haakon Mellemsether or Haagenson; Sivert Aalbu; John Riskaasen; and Jens Rise.

In all there were fifty-two passages bought on the same boat for the same place in America; viz., Yankton, South Dakota. One or two of the group, I believe, went to Brookings, South Dakota, including Mr. Haagenson.

We left these people, while making this digression, on the king's highway severing forever the strong ties that bound them to the land and the people of their birth. As we now resume our journey with them, especially if we have not made the trip before, we are irresistibly attracted by the wild and rugged manifestations of nature along our route. Both the way and its surroundings were prophetic of the much further stretching way to be traversed, often with weary feet, by these people, could they have foreseen it.

The road, tho well built, winds endlessly and often in sharp turns thru the narrow valley between the mountains which in places almost form a gorge. In many places the road is cut out of the solid rock of the mountain side so that on one side is the high and nearly perpendicular cliff; on the other, and only a few feet away, the almost perpendicular descent to the raging, roaring river hundreds of feet below. The sun is only now (April) beginning to reduce the eight months' snow on the mountains. This turns the river in the main valleys, as well as the hundreds of smaller streams coming down the mountain sides, into whitefoamed, tumultuous torrents rolling great stones before them and resounding thru the adjacent valleys and mountain sides with a deep and deafening roar—beware! beware!

Looking up the mountain sides we see pine and evergreen creeping up well toward the top. But while the sides are thus robed in beautiful green, the tops are crowned with the pure white of the "eternal" snows. So here was both music and raiment fit for kings and the sons of Vikings, and these sounds and sights those people never forgot nor could forget.

After a two-day tramp thru the snow and slush we reach the railway station, Storen, fifty miles from our starting point. Here the drivers return and more sad partings and some tears. Fortunately the new sights and experiences now begin to crowd upon the consciousness of these people and help them forget for the time being, just what they most need to forget, what lies behind, if they are to successfully march forward. Most of these people had never before been out of the parish in which they were born or seen a railway or locomotive, not to speak of riding behind one. And being naturally intelligent and forward looking men and women, they took a deep interest in the new world which continually unfolded to them as they journeyed on toward their faroff destination, covering nearly a month of time.

We must now turn to the causes or motives which led these people to undertake this long journey, so full of perils and uncertainties, and also of hardships which can better be imagined than described in detail. Transatlantic travel, forty years ago, was about as different from what it is now as the ox team was different from the automobile.

The causes of this emigration, as one might almost surmise, were both economic and religious. The religious motive was especially apparent as far as the leaders were concerned.

Some years before this migration, a traveling evangelist had come thru Opdal and had held meetings from house to house in the neighborhood where these people lived, the state church building not being open for that sort of religious exercises. His name was Hans Remen, or as he was often called, Hans Romsdalen. He was a giant in physical proportions and also had a moral courage and religious ardor to match his body. He denounced the dead forms of religion current in the Lutheran State Church as of no avail, and worse than nothing, in that they caused people to rest their salvation on a false foundation. He testified by reference to the Bible, and to personal experience, that the only basis of salvation for man was a personal, vital relation to Jesus Christ, entered into by faith; and that in Him alone could man find forgiveness of sin, peace with God, and a good conscience.

The ground was somewhat ready for this sort of seed in that there was a considerable number of people who had come to feel about the State Church, much as the evangelist expressed it. Among them were the leaders of these emigrants, Berhaug Rise (or as the name came to be spelled, Reese), Halvor Hevle, Iver Sneve and Thore Fossem. A revival of religion resulted and there came to be a considerable group of people who sought a more vital religion than what was manifested in the State Church. Thru worship and preaching in private houses, however, they could find an open door and they continued this movement. This religious movement thus gained more and more adherents, so that not only had most of the members of this exodus been touched by it but also many more who were left behind at this time.

It was a foregone conclusion that these lay preachers, especially the above mentioned leaders, would soon find themselves marked for persecution by the representatives of the established church and also by petty government officials who of course stood back of that church organization. Then, too, while looking upon the State Church not only as dead religiously but also as a positive menace to true religion, in that it led people astray, and persecuted those who were trying to lead the way back to the teachings of the lowly Nazarene, yet they were compelled to give a tithe of their principal farm produce toward the upkeep of this institution.

There was much discussion and many clashes between the adherents of the old and the new. But as the chasm seemed to widen, and the hope of vitalizing the State Church from within to lessen, being backed as it was financially and otherwise by the whole machinery of the government, this religious situation and persecution became a strong motive for seeking a freer atmosphere.

Then strongly re-enforcing the religious motive were both the general as also some special economic conditions at this time, which pressed upon these people. As aforesaid, the leaders of this movement had been owners of small and medium sized farms, but with debts on them. Yet under ordinary conditions they could have managed to take care of these obligations, as they were long-time loans and at low rates of interest. But worse than these larger obligations was the fact that some of them had somehow fallen into the hands of the professional loan sharks and usurers of the place. The method of procedure of these parasites was to make short time loans, generally becoming due in the fall of the year, and taking security in the milch cows or grain crop of the small farmers. On the very day of maturity they would demand immediate payment or threaten foreclosure with its attendant expense and annoyance to the borrower. Having bullied and scared their victims into the suitable state of mind they would, with hypocritical pretense of graciousness, offer to compromise by buying the mortgaged property, usually milch cows and seed grain, themselves, thus saving the expense and disgrace of going to law. This was generally accepted and the sale made, but of course at the lender's price. Then in the spring the farmers had to have cows and seed grain to do any business and usually had to buy both back again from these sharks, thus getting into their hands again, and thus the vicious circle continued until the poor borrower was finally worn out and had to give up the struggle.

However, the final blow, economically, which brought the leaders of our party to the great decision of emigrating, was a certain cooperative mercantile enterprise which they had helped to form supposedly for the economic benefit of the community. This was in the early dawn of the cooperative movement in Norway, and these people were quick to see its economic possibilities, but had not yet learned to know and to guard against the many pitfalls which such enterprises have to face and avoid if they are to succeed. And dearly did they pay for their first lesson.

The shares of the company were assessable with unlimited liabilities on the part of the share holder. Thus, of course the business had almost unlimited credit with wholesalers. For a time the organization seemed to prosper. After a while, however, suspicion began to form in the minds of some that things were not just right. An investigation was eventually made. The manager immediately disappeared. The government now stepped in and declared a bankruptcy. The manager, having gotten away beyond recall, the wholesale houses presented bills of all kinds and large amounts for goods which the directors felt certain had never been received. But with the manager absconded the company could not disprove these claims, and the court, belonging socially and politically to the big business class, naturally held the scales of justice, socalled, in favor of the wholesale creditors. The result was that these poor pioneers in the field of economic cooperation found themselves liable and their property attached for as much as 6000% of the face value of their shares. It goes without saying that the government officials saw to it that they themselves got their utmost limit out of the general slaughter. Berhaug Rise and a couple of other victims appealed to the courts against the high handed work of the big business concerns, and the petty government officials involved, but lost the case, and all that they had was attached and ordered sold.

Finding revealed thru all this procedure the persecution both of the civil and the ecclesiastical authorities, and seeing no chance at that point of either religious or economic betterment for themselves and their children, they came to the great decision to try their fortunes in the far-away land of which they had heard many and strange tales. For them, as for so many others of every race and tongue, this far-away land was the land of their dreams; the land of the true where they could live anew; where the song birds dwell; the land of promise, and also of fulfillment, of hitherto crushed hopes and thwarted aspirations.

Returning now to follow our party from Trondhjem, where we left them, to Yankton, South Dakota, we find that the journey was mostly the uneventful, uncomfortable one which was the lot of immigrants of forty years ago, or early '80's. There was much sea sickness and much loathing and disgust with the food and accommodations, both of such a quality as they had never experienced before. Fortunately most of them had food of their own.

The nearest to any mishap to any of the party fell to the lot of the writer of this chronicle, who was a boy of six years. It happened in the awful throng and confusion of Castle Garden, the old landing place of immigrants at New York City. I was committed to the care of a certain servant girl of the family, there being four other children to be kept track of by father and mother. But in the noise and confusion of embarking on certain transports taking us to the railway on the main land, she seems to have lost her head as well as her charge, and I recall that I found myself wandering alone among the vast spaces of Castle Garden and the docks. I was crying because of the loss of father, mother, and all my friends, and searching for them in vain. At length some sort of official discovered me and after some questioning he joined me in the search. We went out on some boats, I recall, where people were embarking, and he inquired everywhere if anyone had lost a boy. I recall very vividly how a woman at one place claimed me as her very own and how I protested with more vehemence than politeness. The official took my view of the case. We continued our search and at last we met Father, who by this time had discovered my absence and started out to search. Needless to say, there was more joy over my return than over the four other children who had not strayed away.

Thus the transportation company at length was enabled to carry out its contract of delivering the same number of heads at Yankton as it took on at Trondhjem. And they did it much in the same matter-of-fact and impersonal way as a railroad company undertakes to deliver so many head of cattle at the stockyards of Chicago.—All the honor to them that they deserved!

Chapter VII
Landing At Yankton And Getting On The Land

It may be of interest to take a look at the town of Yankton of forty years ago, where we finally landed. Yankton was the terminal of this division of the C.M. & St. P. Railway, or, as it was then called, the Dakota Southern. It was also the capitol city of Dakota Territory comprising the present states of North and South Dakota. Its buildings were mostly small wooden houses, but, as may be surmised, it commanded a large trade territory, for besides being the end of the railway it was touched by a considerable steamboat traffic up and down the river and had considerable Indian trade, besides that of the adjacent white settlements. So it was then the most important city in the Dakotas and had been decidedly so before that time.

Here the immigrants were given a cordial welcome and temporary shelter at the home of Mrs. Carrie Severson, a widow whom they had known from the old country. We do not know, of course, how our fathers and mothers felt about the enterprise by this time, but to us youngsters, who as yet were not loaded with the burdens of life, the green grass and the freedom to scamper about seemed good after a whole month's confinement in a crowded steerage and more crowded railway coaches.

Next day friends of the party, who had immigrated some ten years before, came with teams and wagons to help these newer comers to get on the land and make their start in the new and, to these people, strange land. For this was indeed a very different country from the one they had left and even from the picture many of them had had in mind. There was much to learn and many disappointments at first as we shall see.

Among the men who undertook to receive this large company in their homes and to help them get established in homes of their own, and who extended the glad hand of welcome that day, should be mentioned these: Stingrim Hinseth, Ingebricht Fagerhaugh, Haldo Saether, John Rye, John Aalbu and Halvor Hinseth. These men loaded into their lumber wagons the big blue chests and smaller parcels; deposited the passengers as best they could and started out over the prairie on what was called "The Sioux Falls Trail". This trail angled all the way to their homes in Turkey Creek, over twenty miles to the northeast. Darkness soon overtook the travelers and the following circumstance created considerable merriment for the hosts, at least. The newcomers observed, as they journeyed on thru the darkness, very many gleams of light as it were from innumerable human habitations. These points of light were, of course, fire flies, so called, or certain phosphorescent bugs which at that time were very numerous because of the abundant grass prevailing everywhere. At length one of the passengers remarked in evident astonishment! "This country must be very thickly populated, judging by the many lights we see"! When daylight came, however, the lights and most of the supposed inhabitants had utterly disappeared.

It may be of some interest to the new and coming generations to take a look at the country around Turkey Creek as it greeted the curious gaze of these new comers of forty years ago on that first morning of their arrival. Most of the friends who brought them out from town and distributed them for temporary shelter were settled on the Turkey Creek bottom and located about where they or their dwellings are now. Farthest north up the valley was John Rye, then Halvor Hinseth, next Steingrim Hinseth, I. Fagerhaug, Ole Solem and Jens Eggen, in order as named. But back of the creek bottom where these earliest homesteaders had located was the far stretching open prairie—a sea of waving grass—with a lonely dug-out only here and there and vast stretches of "no man's land" between.

There were no regular highways, only some trails winding their way over the endless grass, in some general direction, but with many crooks and turns to avoid a hill, ravine or slough. These sloughs, or small lakes, were very numerous and of considerable size and depth in those days. There is today many a waving field of corn and grain where we boys of the first generation of settlers once launched our home made boats, hunted ducks, swam and occasionally came near drowning.

The best travelled of the trails in the part of the country we are describing was the old territorial trail called the Sioux Falls Road. This angled in a north-easterly direction all the way from Yankton to Sioux Falls, and many a prairie schooner could be seen moving with stately slowness over this road, not to speak of other vehicles which were numerous. As a boy I have seen long caravans of Indians, perhaps twenty or thirty teams in a string, trekking over this road. When the ruts became too deep, by reason of much travel and the action of the water, another trail would be made close alongside the old. Thus in places six or eight pairs of ruts, made by many wagons and feet, could be seen side by side.

There were no wire fences to mark boundaries between farms or to form pastures in those days, and the cattle were herded far and wide. The people in the Turkey Creek Valley herded as far as Clay Creek. The writer of this, altho not of the earliest herd boys of the time, and living near Turkey Creek, has taken his herd many a day to the proximity of Clay Creek with practically open pasture all the way.

I am speaking for many boys and some girls, too, of those days, boys and girls who are fathers and mothers now, when I say that our pasture fence was Clay Creek on the west and Turkey Creek on the east. Not that we were not free to go farther but that the day was not long enough to get any farther and back again the same day.

There was at this time, when our pilgrims arrived, but very little of the ground broken up. What little there was broken was mostly on the creek bottom, but scarcely any on the upland. And when a little later patches of prairie were broken up in order to comply with the homestead law requirements for getting title to the land, these patches were usually in a draw or low-lying strip between the hills. Thus the fields of early days were not laid out with any reference to north or south, but their direction was determined entirely by the hills and valleys. The little breaking which was done was done with oxen and sometimes the direction of the field to be was determined by the oxen themselves more than by the driver. Some wheat, corn and oats was raised, but the main dependence of the farmer was cattle and milking.

The dwellings were of three main types. There was the dug-out, usually in a side-hill, with a sod roof, a few studdings and boards being used to support the roof. The walls and floor were usually the native earth. The sod house was a more advanced and perhaps more stylish dwelling. Closely related to the sod house was the mud house where the walls, about two or three feet thick, were made of well tramped mud and straw. These mud houses were at times whitewashed and were both comfortable and sightly. As for comfort in the cold winter the dug-out and sod house were not so bad when properly built. But do not imagine that they were equal to your furnace-heated, modern house. They were, after all, a temporary hole in the ground to preserve life until houses could be had. A house made of lumber was a luxury which many an early settler had to look forward to for many a hard, long year, and often he had to die in the dug-out or sod shanty. Finally, there was the story-and-a-half frame house of two or three rooms with a possible lean-to. This type of house put one in the class of the most well-to-do; and such a habitation was the hope and dream of years for many a pilgrim mother of those days.

We have turned aside from our main narrative for a look at the country as it appeared to our band of pilgrims as they looked about them on that first morning of their arrival in the Turkey Creek Valley. And the view was not all that they had hoped for. What could these men—farmers and men of trades—do in this howling wilderness of grass, grass and nothing but grass? Yes, there was something else—mosquitoes—and oh, how they stung! Also flies, and how incessantly and mercilessly they attacked the fair soft skin of these pilgrims from the Norseland! Finally, there was the heat, which literally took the fair skin off their faces in flakes and put on a tan which made them almost unrecognizable.

Moreover, what could these shoemakers, masons, painters or even farmers do here? Shoes were bought; houses were of sod or earth and needed no paint; years would be required to make cultivated fields out of this sea of grass, and meanwhile they and their families must somehow live.

The kind hosts did all they could to encourage and make comfortable the newcomers, sharing with them what accommodations they had. But we must remember that these first comers had not been here long themselves. The dwellings were small, without cooling porches, and in summer necessarily hot, and they had no screens to protect the inmates from the blood-thirsty fly and mosquito. So there was but little rest or comfort by day or night, especially for those unused to these conditions. This together with the unaccustomed food, which at first completely upset them, made some of the newcomers very discouraged with the new country.

One of these "blue" ones said to Father soon after their arrival: "Do you suppose you will ever get your money back which you loaned us for our passage?" "That," replied father, "I do not know. But this I do know, that now I have no money either to take myself or any of you back again." "Then," rejoined the first one, "if now I could stand on the highway where we started, even with nothing but a shirt on my back, I should be the happiest man alive." Another said: "There is not even grass here such as one can cut with a scythe and, as for land I shall have none of it." And in his case it became so. He never homesteaded and later worked at his trade in Yankton and Sioux City, where he died many years later.

Father tried to take a brighter view and to cheer those complaining ones and said to Iver Sneve, who had just expressed the wish to be back on the old sod: "In three years you will be butchering your own pork, raised on your farm in this new land." Then Iver broke out into his characteristically loud, uproarious laughter, full of incredulity and almost scorn, and said: "Berhaug Rise, I have up till this time considered you a man of sense and good judgment, but now I am compelled to believe that your mind's eye is shimmering. I cannot even *keep alive* for *three years* in this man-consuming wilderness. Unless some one takes pity on me and helps me to return home, the flies and mosquitoes alone will have finished me before that time. Oh, that some of us older men could have had sense enough to return even when we were as far as England," he added. This is a sample of many conversations, and these expressions were by no means uttered as jokes either. Nevertheless, this Iver Sneve lived some 35 years after this conversation and was worth $25,000.00 when he died.

However, these people were here and, with all bridges burned behind them, they realized that mere lamentations would not meet the situation. Something must be done to live and to keep their families, here or in the old country, as was the case with some, alive. So in a few days a party of the younger men set out afoot toward the present site of Parker to seek work on the railroad which was just being extended from that point westward toward Mitchell. They found work with shovel and pick. But ten hours a day, in the hot sun and with an Irish boss over them to see that these implements kept constantly moving, was no soft initiation for these fair skinned men just out of a much colder climate. However, with true Norse and immigrant grit they "stuck it out" and earned a little money before the first winter of 1880-1 came on.

Berhaug Rise and Halvor Hevle, by the help of the good neighbors, got some lumber hauled from Vermilion, the latter for a dug-out and the former for a frame house 14 × 16 and 12 feet high. This house was built by John Rye and is still standing in the old homestead after nearly forty years. In this house made of one thickness of drop siding and paper, we spent the terrible snow winter of 80-81. It was the winter of the great blizzard which came in the middle of October. And the deep snow never left until nearly the middle of April, when the big flood of 1881 resulted. Luckily Father had filed without ever seeing it, as also Grandma, on some land traversed by deep ravines. There had been heavy hardwood timber in these ravines, but it was now cut, with nothing left but young shoots—brush—and great stumps, some 4-6 feet in diameter. These stumps formed the winter's fuel, as also most of the winter's work. With such a house it became necessary to keep the stove about red hot in cold weather to have any comfort and, of course, everything froze solid during the nights. But if it had not been for the old oaken stumps and the warm woolen clothes we had brought with us, it is hard to see how we could have survived that first winter. Much better off, as far as the cold was concerned, were those who had a good dugout. But by a sort of special dispensation of providence there was no sickness requiring a doctor in our family or in the neighborhood. And this was well, for doctors were far away and expensive to get. We children waded and coasted in the deep snow, getting hands and feet thoroly wet, but never had a better time in our lives, as far as I can recall. There was yet no public school in that neighborhood, so there was lots of time for play—mostly coasting down the surrounding hillsides.

A word ought also to be said about the outbuildings, if we may call them such, for they were typical of what many others had. The stable, for three cows and two ponies, was an excavation in the side hill. The hill formed the full wall on the upper side and part of the wall on the other sides, the rest being filled in with straw, hay or sod. Over these walls was thrown brush with a little frame work of supports underneath, and then the whole was covered with hay or straw. For a door, in our case, Father took a bush, covered with an entanglement of grape vines, set it in the doorway and piled hay against it. This last, however, was an emergency measure as the notorious blizzard of 1880 above referred to, broke upon us before the structure was quite finished. But as there were many emergency appliances in those days, of every kind, this one was nothing out of the ordinary.

The place where the two pigs were kept was built on the same plan, only that it was divided into two stories—the chickens having roosts over the pigs. But this combination did not prove a success, for whenever the chickens fell down or ventured down to their room mates below, they were eaten up by the pigs.

Perhaps a word should also be said about two of the inmates of the stable, for they also were common types of those and even much later times. These were two Texas ponies which Father and Halvor Hevle had purchased out of a herd driven to Yankton. After picking their choices out of the herd in a large corral, and paying $20.00 apiece for their choices, the men in charge lassoed the animals and turned them over to the new owners, at the end of a fairly long new rope. It was well that the ropes were new and fairly long, for it took three days of both brave and skilled maneuvering to get these wild animals of the plains to the home of their new masters. And the masters were certainly tired and not over-enthusiastic over their new horse power when they at last arrived. Matters were not so serene as could be wished while these little savages were being picketed outside. But when winter came and the animals which had never known any roof lower than the blue sky, nor walls more confining than the far-flung horizon, were to be quartered in a hole in the ground, real excitement began. Whenever any one ventured into the stable he would no sooner open the door than he would see these creatures on their haunches trying to jump thru the roof, which feat they almost succeeded in accomplishing. At first it was a problem how to get near enough to tend to them. The hay could be poked down the roof to where their heads ought to be, but the water was not so easy. In spite of precaution they "got the drop" on Father once I recall, and he was in bed for some time, but lucky to escape with his life. It should be said to their credit, however, that by the help of Lars Almen, above referred to, they were in due time subdued and served many years, and faithfully, according to their size and strength, with only an occasional runaway. These wild horses filled a useful place in the needs of these scattered beginners far from each other and from towns. But it was after all the ox who really helped subdue the soil and lay the foundations for farming and prosperity in general. But for the people we are now describing real farming had not yet begun, so more of that a little later.

Chapter VIII
The Pioneer Mothers And Their Part In The Struggle

What we have said of the pioneers so far has reflected for the most part what the pioneer fathers said, did or thought. If any one should get the impression from this seemingly one-sided treatment that pioneer mothers bore any lesser part of the burdens and sacrifices incident to leaving the land of their birth, and beginning all over again the long struggle of re-establishing themselves, and that, too, on the bare prairie where there was absolutely nothing to begin with, such a one has been greatly misled. While the work, not to speak of the privations and feelings of our mothers, is more difficult to record on paper, it is not one whit less real or deserving of any less appreciation. We can only give a few outlines picturing their part of the life. Yet if any one has a little imagination he can easily fill in the picture with its various tints and shades. The shadows were often both deep and tragic.

For a woman, even more than for a man, the social ties of life mean a great deal. Our mothers left their home relations, kindred and neighbors close around them, to be set down on a lonely prairie, cut off from all the dear relationships of childhood and womanhood. Even where there were neighbors, or soon came to be, they were at first strangers and often spoke a strange tongue. So for them there were many long days and weary years of isolation and heart hunger for those whom they had known and loved long ago, but now could never again see.

Then, too, they had left homes, some of them very comfortable homes, where they had always had the necessary equipment for ordinary housekeeping. Here for years they had to do with little and in many lines nothing. The average newcomer's larder from which our mothers had to get the materials for three meals a day was generally confined to these articles: Corn meal with more or less of wheat flour, often less, and not seldom none at all; fat salt pork, at least part of the time; milk in considerable quantity both for cooking, drinking in place of tea or coffee and for making a number of dishes made almost exclusively from milk. Butter they generally had, but as that was about the only thing they had to sell it had to be conserved and lard or a mixture of lard and molasses used instead. There were eggs, or came to be, but while used more or less, they, too, had to go toward getting such few groceries as could be afforded. These were coffee, sugar, a little kerosene for one small lamp, and last, but, for many of the men, not least—tobacco. Now let no pink tea scion or descendant of these men who had to be the breaking plows of our new state, hold up lilly fingered hands of horror at this last and often not least item in the grocery list of that day. For if you are a man child of this stock and you had been there and then, with all the physical discomforts of the climate, lack of suitable clothes and food, not to speak of the frequently loathsome drinking water, you might have felt justified in the use of a nerve sedative too. It shall be said to their credit, too, that while most of the men of that day used the weed, few of them used it in such beastly excess as is often seen today. But rightly or wrongly, they thought they had to have it. Thus Lars Almen, when he arrived at Yankton, had 50 cents in money left. He started to invest that last mite of the family resources in tobacco. His wife remonstrated, saying it would be more fitting to get a few provisions such as they could all partake of. The ever undaunted Lars replied: "If I have tobacco I know I can do something or other to make us a living, but if I have no tobacco I can do nothing". So he bought tobacco, and he also made good on the "living." Forgetting, then, the last named item in on the list of staple provisions, we find that salt pork, usually fried, corn meal in some form, such as mush or bread, more or less of wheat flour and milk or some dish made out of milk in whole or part, were the resources out of which our pioneer mothers had to provide three palatable meals a day, summer and winter. This is not saying that these materials were always abundant, but rather that it was these or nothing. There were, of course, special occasions when a little pastry in the shape of home made cookies or fried cakes was on the table, but cake and pie and such like luxuries were not often seen the first years.

The fuel with which to prepare this food was, for most of them, hay, or in summer cow chips, and later on, when they began to raise corn, corn cobs. But hay was the principal fuel, and huge piles of it were required to do much cooking or for heating. For, as can be readily seen, one had to keep stuffing it into the stove almost continually to get any hot fire. Picture to yourself then a room—sod house, dugout or a frame house about 12 × 14 which was kitchen, sitting room, bedroom, and everything else combined. The hay, as was the case in winter time, would cover a large part of the floor and, of course, raise continual dust. The stove would get full of ashes in a short time, and if the hay was damp would, of course, smoke more or less. In such a place, with such conveniences and out of such materials, our pioneer mothers had to solve the problem of three meals a day and do all their other work besides. In summer, of course, it was not quite so bad, as they usually had a lean to or cook shanty of some sort, for use in warm weather. Is it strange that many of these women who came to find a new and, as they supposed, a better home, found instead an early grave, and what was worse, some even lost their minds? The men could get away, at least to be outdoors a part of the time, but the women had to live and move and have their whole being in these surroundings and conditions. So let us not fail to speak the word of appreciation to those of them who are still living or to cherish the memory of those who have made their final pilgrimage. So let there be flowers and kind words for the living and flowers and tears for the dead. For our pioneer mothers gave more for us than we can ever know.

Chapter IX
Indians As Occasional Guests And Visitors

While still speaking of life and conditions in the Turkey Creek Valley and surrounding country as it was during the winter of eighty and eighty one, and even later, I ought to mention our occasional Indian visitors. They used to travel thru that country in considerable numbers at that time over the Sioux Falls road already mentioned. As a boy I have seen possibly twenty or thirty teams in a single procession. They sometimes camped near the brush bordering the ravine which was close by our house. The women would excavate the snow, sometimes several feet deep, and pitch the tepees, while the children scampered around them on the snow bank. The following incident may not be out of place as showing the heartaches and difficulties for the Indian incident to his transition from the free life of the plains to that of civilization. One day an Indian family consisting of a man and wife with some children, as also an old squaw which was evidently the grandmother of the children, camped near our house. The man and the younger squaw were trying to boil their kettle in the camp fire while the old squaw went out into the adjoining gulches, presumably to dig roots or hunt. The pot did not boil very fast and Father, by signs, invited them to come into the house and boil their pot. They seemed perfectly willing to do this, and coming inside they sat around our fire with the pot on the stove. But in a little while the old squaw returned, and not seeing her children by the fire where all good Indians would be supposed to be, she suspected something wrong and came into the house where she found her degenerate offspring located as above described. We could not, of course, understand the words she said, but we could easily make out that she was not complimenting them any on their new-found quarters, for the language was very emphatic and her face stern. She also got some immediate action. Having scolded them soundly for forsaking the firesides and ways of their fathers to enter the lodges of the palefaces, she snatched the kettle from the stove and walked out followed by the now chastened son and daughter with their children.

We had many visits from the Indians and they never did us any harm. However, I suspect that they were more welcome to us youngsters than to our mothers who never seemed quite at ease with them.

Most of those who came thru the country at that time had wagons. But some used the travaux, consisting of two rails lashed to the saddle of the pony, one on each side, and crosspieces behind the horse with blankets or skins covering. The ends of the rails, of course, slid on the ground. On this rude contrivance the Indian loaded his few belongings, sometimes the squaw and children, and journeyed over the country.

Chapter X
The Great Snow Winter of 1880-1 and the Great Flood Of 1881—Building A Boat

We have already referred to this winter of 80-81 as the terrible snow winter. May we add a few words on that in order to understand what followed in the spring.

The snow, a three days' snow storm or blizzard, came on October 15th, and the snow never left, but kept piling up without thawing out to any extent until April. Railroad connection with the outer world, as far as the few towns in the state were concerned, was cut off, completely in many instances, after the 1st of January. This, of course, made coal as well as other provisions unobtainable in many cases. The people in some towns, as for instance Watertown, had to take what they could find to preserve life. So many empty buildings and other property made of wood were taken for fuel.

In the outlying country places the settlers could not get to them, even when some provisions were available. In not a few cases, too, there was nothing to sell and no money for buying. So barred by one or all of the circumstances, the settlers had to get along and try to preserve life as best they could. As for the few groceries which they might ordinarily have used, they dispensed even with them for the most part. Many lived on corn meal, ground on the coffee mill. But there was one privation which for many proved the "unkindest cut of all"—tobacco. Many and sore were the lamentations because of the lack of this one commodity and many the devices to get it. A man can live without coffee, sugar and wheat-bread, not to speak of less necessary things, but tobacco—well, you can't do anything more to him after that.

As can easily be seen, when this vast quantity of snow began to go out, especially going out so late in the spring, it created a flood. Every creek became a raging river, the rivers became more like vast moving lakes. So if communication with towns had been difficult before it became well nigh impossible now. The whole Missouri bottom, for instance, became one vast and roaring sea, coming up to the bluffs of the present Mission Hill and

Volin. But yet, can such a little thing as fourteen miles of roaring water and floating debris stand between a man and his tobacco, or a woman and her cup of coffee, especially when the latter is the only thing approaching a luxury that she has? No! By the shades of all our Viking ancestors, No! After looking over their possible resources of men and materials for the undertaking of defying the angry flood, they found that Ole Solem, who then lived on Turkey Creek, had a few remnants of lumber. They also found that Anders Oien had had a little experience in boat building, and Ole Johnson was an ex-fisherman and thus could row a boat if they had one. So with the help of those mentioned and others, such as Ingebricht Fagerhaug, who was a carpenter, and Steingrim Hinseth, the boat was built. It was crude, of course, and leaky, yet counted seaworthy because the situation was getting desperate. It should be said in fairness that mere personal and private needs were not the only motive with these men. For instance, some of the leaders of this enterprise, like Solem and Fagerhaug, had no need or use for tobacco, but needing other things and realizing the general needs they joined with heart and hand.

When the craft was finished Steingrim Hinseth hauled the boat and the men, Ole Solem, Ingebricht Fagerhaug, Thore Fossem and, I believe, Ole Johnson, to the foot of the bluffs, a couple of miles northwest of Volin, where the boat was launched. The cargo was all that the little craft could carry, consisting of very many different parcels of butter and some eggs. These, belonging to many different parties and being the only things they had to sell, were to be exchanged for a few necessities such as mentioned above.

When the cargo was all in and the crew embarked there was about two inches left of the boat above the water line and the boat a little leaky besides. But with true Viking spirit they struck out over the twelve or fourteen miles of angry flood towards Yankton. There they were able to do the necessary shopping for the whole neighborhood, and in three days from the time of starting they were back without mishap and all errands carried out. It goes without saying that they were welcomed by the many expectant ones in the whole neighborhood and that there was great rejoicing on the part of both men and women, for the women got their coffee and the men got—well—whatever was coming to them.

Chapter XI
Beginning Their Real Struggle With The Earth

The long and memorable winter of '80-'81 had at last come to an end. The resulting flood, too, as in the time of Noah, at length subsided, and now our new comers must begin their first real struggle with the earth in the new land. Without tools or draught animals, and even any knowledge of farming conditions on this new soil, and without means to buy tools, this struggle became for many both hard and prolonged. They had had during the winter their baptism in self-denial and privation. They were now to learn further that while the new land might possibly flow with milk and honey, yet if it was to flow for them, they would have to do the milking and gather the honey.

As an illustration of how the struggle in subduing the soil began for these people, may I again refer to my Father as an illustration of many others. I refer to him merely because I can recall these circumstances better in his case than in that of others and, also because the experiences of others were similar and in many cases much worse.

He had hired a man to break five acres the first summer. This was an ordinary amount of plow land, largely because the government required this much to be broken in order to comply with the homestead regulations. During the winter he had made a small harrow and in the spring sowed most of this ground to wheat and tried the best he could to harrow it with the ponies already mentioned. The year was not very favorable, as I can recall it, and with such equipment the results can be surmised. I do not recall just what they were, but I am quite sure we did not eat much wheat flour the following winter. He had one acre of corn, which he worked with the hoe. He bought, like most of the others, or, rather went into debt for, a pair of steers that spring. These he, with the help of Lars Almen, who worked together with him, as also Halvor Hevle, tried to "break" for work purposes. These animals proved themselves notoriously stubborn and fractious and made their drivers earn most of what they got out of them in the way of work. This, however, may have been due to the inexperience of the drivers. For, as already said, the ox, next to the cow, was the beginner's best friend, and without him it is hard to see how the pioneers could have gotten along at all. To be sure, some of these animals did not take kindly to the yoke and many were the scrapes they got their owners into, running away and breaking up both wagons and tools. Yet when you consider the lot of the ox you cannot be too hard on him for his occasional bad humor. As a boy I have driven him many a day, and often lost my patience with him, for which I now humbly apologize. We worked him on the plow, both stubble and breaking plow, drag, stoneboat and the heaviest work that was to be done. At noon or night we unyoked him and let him go to get a little grass or hay for himself. No oats for him, only the long kind you administer with a whip; no thanks to him when the long, hot day of pulling a breaking plow at last is done, but very likely a parting kick. We have not given the ox his well-earned place among the foundation builders of our land, and I propose that even at this late date we should repent and build in South Dakota a monument to the ox, our early, faithful and indispensable friend.

The first few years after arriving were required by our pioneers for making temporary shelters for themselves and their few animals; also in providing some way of obtaining the bare necessities of life while they could lay the foundations for a larger prosperity and more comforts. As already indicated, the first resource and dependence for getting a little money was eggs, butter and hay. These commodities were sold to get the few groceries and small necessities which they could not well do without. Some of the men worked out to supplement their meager income.

By 1885, roughly speaking, these hardy men really began to wrestle with the soil in earnest and thus make possible something more than a bare existence. From about '83 to '90 a picturesque and ever recurring scene, when spring and early summer came, was the breaking rig moving slowly but majestically over the long furrows. There were from four to six oxen to each plow and most generally it took two men to hold the plow and keep the oxen in the straight and narrow way. The country I am describing was very stony and there was many a hard lift and aching back before these stones could be pried out of the ground and hauled away sufficiently to make breaking possible. Even after spending many weeks at this clearing work there would still be many stones left which the plow would strike with such violence as to almost fell the man at the handles. With the plow out of the ground and the load suddenly lightening the oxen would make the most of this relief by starting on a trot so that often the plow could not be gotten back into the sod for a rod or two. Two neighbors would often go in together in breaking, each furnishing one yoke of oxen.

This sod would be put into corn or flax the first season and the next into wheat. The returns were generally quite meager compared with what that ground is producing now. But even a little meant much then. Drought was the principal drawback. Then, too, these early beginners did not have the modern machinery either for putting in, harvesting or threshing grain, and this fact was also a large cause for small yields. However, they kept on breaking up a little more each year, and after a few years the ground was subdued enough to begin to raise corn and consequently hogs. The beef cattle as a source of income had been good earlier, but the price of cattle went so low during this period that there was not much inducement. Then, too, as the country came to be settled and broken there was less possibility of keeping herds of cattle. I recall that during this depression in the latter eighties good milch cows sold for $10.00-$15.00 and other cattle in proportion. Of course, in the panic or notorious depression of 93-4, even grain and hogs went down with everything else. Corn was sold for eight cents per bushel and wheat as low as 35-40 cents. But generally speaking, in the period we are describing, when these path-finders were laying the foundations for permanent homes and farm equipment, corn and hogs became their corner stone of prosperity, with milk and butter a close second.

There arose an industry in the latter '90's which came to be of considerable economic importance—the creamery. These men at first located a considerable distance away and the cream had to be transported in hired wagons. Some of these creameries "failed" and left the farmers to whistle for their long expected and much needed cream checks. Later a co-operative creamery was organized and successfully operated by Sven Vognild on the S. Hinseth place. This was the first real co-operative enterprise in the vicinity.

Returning to early farm conditions, we find that for several years many of the new settlers did not have enough grain to have a threshmachine on the place, but hauled what little they might have to some nearby machine.

As can be seen, there was not much grain to be sold for some time for these farmers. Butter and eggs, and, a little later, cattle, were the chief products which could bring a little ready money. To this should be added hay, which many hauled to Yankton with oxen, getting $2.50-$3.00 per ton. Even at this price, and with such slow transportation, this hay traffic was for many the chief source of any money, and some spent most of the fall and winter months at this work when travel was possible.

Chapter XII
A Bird's Eye View of the Country as it Appeared In 1800-3

We ought, at this point, to make a visit around the neighborhood as it appeared from '81-'83 and even much later. Beginning in the Turkey Creek Valley, we have already indicated the half dozen families which had located there in the early seventies. As we have spoken in another chapter of this earlier wave of pioneer immigrants, I shall pass them by now as also those of that same group who had settled to the south, toward what is now Volin.

Berhaug Rise moved his living house from where it was first placed, viz., one quarter mile west of Ole Solem's, to about one mile west, that is, from the creek bottom at the junction of the ravines which traversed the place from east to west, to the higher land at the head of these ravines.

To the southwest of our place, about a mile distant, was John Johnson, who had settled there in '74 and lived in a log house. To the west one mile was Ole Johnson, who had filed in '79 and was living in a dugout with his family. Another mile or so still farther southwest was Peter Moen, also living in a dugout and having a considerable family. Then going back to Ole Johnson and going north were Peter Johnson, Jonas Vaabeno, Ole Liabo, and John Moene. To the east of Peter Johnson there was in 1880 a man by the name of Roser who, however, left about that time. All of these, as far as I remember, lived in dugouts, with the exception of the first named, who lived in a loghouse.

Going from five to six miles to the northwest of this Turkey Creek settlement, we find another group of pioneers, some of whom had come before 1880 and others a little later. We can mention a few. There was Cornelius Nilsen, Albert Boe, Peter, Albert, and O.O. Gorseth; O. Lokken; Steen Bakke, Mrs. Mary Boe, the Simonson Brothers—Halvor and Ole. Also Asle Mikkelson. There may have been others, but these comprise practically all who were there at that time. The sons and daughters of many of these are either on the old places or in the vicinity to this day. Of course, some have moved away to other parts. Most of these pioneers are still living, but no longer in the dug-outs.

Going west to what was called the West Prairie, about six miles, could be found H. Hagen, the Gustads, Stoems, Skaaness and others. These had come in the earlier wave of immigration which we have mentioned already, i.e. in the early '70's or later '60's.

Going back to our starting point near Turkey Creek and going south, after passing John Johnson already mentioned, we find next the Lawrence place, now owned by Mr. Axlund; then Hans Dahl, followed in order by Haldo Sether, Ole Bjerke, Lars Aaen and the Hoxeng Brothers, both of them then living on the old home place now occupied by Thore Hoxeng. There were, of course, others scattered on either side of this line of settlers, but these were a sort of land marks in the early eighties.

Finally, going some eight miles north from our starting point, we find these: Thore Fossem and Iver Sneve of our original party and a few others like Ole Brunswick, Ingebricht Saatrum and John Rye, whom we have already mentioned, and J. Larsen. The next to the last named and a few others had settled in that vicinity before 1880. Here should also be mentioned the Durums, Baks, Snoens, Ressels, Grudts, and Lees. The old homesteaders of this group too, have for the most part found a last resting place in the neighborhood cemetery. Their children, however, are in most cases to be found on the old place or near by.

I am conscious that this rough sketch of our neighbors and neighboring settlements of 1880-'1 is far from complete. Yet it gives a fair idea of the population over the prairie there at that time. There were magnificent distances between neighbors and settlements. Yet there was often more neighborliness and sociability than in later years. We needed each other then, in fact could not well get along without helping and being helped in various ways by one another. Now we can help ourselves or rather think we can. But really we cannot, and if we of the newer generations lose the old neighborliness we shall be poorer and unhappier in our steam heated, electric lighted houses and swift speeding automobiles than they were with their earth cellars and ox teams and lumber wagons. So let us cherish and keep alive the old neighborly kindness and great-hearted hospitality. Practically all these early settlers at first lived in a one-room dwelling, seldom over 12

× 14 or 16, and this dwelling was in most cases a dugout. Yet in spite of this fact and of having large families of their own to accommodate, the traveler or stranger was not turned out into the night, and the visitor was always welcomed. There was always room, not merely for one more but for half a dozen more if necessary. There never was any lack of room then. In honor of this splendid trait of our pioneer fathers and mothers, let us reserve a room in our big house and, better still, in our hearts, for the occasional stranger or friend, and in doing so we too shall find that while we may not always have "entertained angels unawares", yet by doing so the angels have somehow entertained us more than they otherwise could.

Chapter XIII
The Annual Prairie Fires—The Terror Of The Settlers

During this decade of getting the ground ready and gradually getting an equipment for real farming there was one great enemy which was a continual menace and terror to the homesteaders—the semi-annual burning of the prairie. From times immemorial, before the White settler came, the prairie fire had stalked in majestic splendor over the vast and boundless sea of grass, covering this and adjoining states, licking up with his red and cruel tongue everything before him and leaving a barren desolation behind him. Sometimes set by the lightning, or Indians, or the campfire of the early explorer or trader, this fire, driven by the wind, would meander back and forth over the prairie for days and weeks until rain or a considerable stream might at last stay his stride.

With the first influx of the settler the fire menace greatly multiplied, for not understanding the nature of this menace, they themselves unintentionally set many of these fires. Thus there came to be a fairly certain expectation on the part of the homesteaders of a visit from this monster twice a year—spring and fall—unless he made a clean sweep in the fall, which was not generally the case.

As a boy I recall waking up at night and seeing a strange glare against the window, and upon looking out, I saw a great wave of fire, a moving wall of flame, pass by our house and going on to the south.

Let me give a brief sketch of one of these fires, well remembered by the old settlers and reported to me by H.B. Reese, who was then old enough to be out with the men on the fire fighting line. I give it largely in his own words.

It was Good Friday, 1887. In the morning we noticed smoke in the northwest. There was also a strong wind from that direction. There had just previously been several days of wind as also sunshine, so everything was dry as tinder. We knew at once what the black flag, hoisted to the sky in the northwest meant. It meant a challenge from the Fire King to come out and fight for our own and our neighbors' homes—buildings, stock and everything we had that could burn. We hurriedly got our weapons of sacks and water ready and started out to meet the giant and offer him all the resistance we could. But our antagonist was terribly swift as well as strong, and when we reached Jonas Vaabeno's place, three miles to the northwest, he had already done his terrible work, making a clean sweep of all outbuildings, mostly made of hay or straw, as also of the dugout which served for a dwelling. Where the stable had stood were the remnants of some half-burnt cattle. We hurried on to Peter Johnson's, but the Fire Demon was victorious and took everything except the dugout dwelling. The same fate was dealt out to Ole Liabo farther north. We were now driven back on our own home premises, and after desperate efforts we saved our buildings, but, of course, had to surrender everything not on the premises where the buildings were, such as trees, hay, etc. When night came and we could return to the house we just threw ourselves flat on the floor completely exhausted, not having tasted food during the whole day.

Next day, looking out over the country to the northwest, we could see very little except a vast desolation—how far no one seemed to know—of blackened prairie, dotted with many ashpiles which in many cases, as tho they were tombstones, marked the graves of all the settlers' material possessions except the land and a few cattle. It is a puzzle to know how they managed to keep these cattle with the prairie burned off, but they did. Not only that, but tho sorely tried, yet not broken in will or spirit, they borrowed money, even at outrageous interest rates, rebuilt their temporary shelters and began the struggle once more from the bottom up.

The last and most terrible of all the fires, as far as known, swept over that country only two years later, 1889. As the writer of this was old enough to be an active participant in connection with this, I recall it vividly. The day was in early spring and began very hazy with so much smoke in the atmosphere that one could not see much beyond half a mile. There was a strong wind from the northwest, such as was common in spring in those days, and the prairie grass was thoroly dried out and very abundant. This condition, however, was not unusual in the spring of the year. On coming out after dinner I noticed that the haze or smoke seemed thicker toward the northwest than in other directions. On looking more closely I soon saw whirls of smoke rolling up toward the sky. I immediately gave the alarm, and every one at the house, including mother, rushed out to meet the foe. We did not have to go far before we met him, and so swiftly did he come that in our hasty retreat toward the house Mother was very nearly overcome by the smoke and heat. Fortunately there was a piece of plowed ground near by where she was able to find safety and lie down until sufficiently recovered to go on to the house. Then we all took our stand, some hauling water, others fighting at the front. There was a strip of plowed ground, or fire break, around the place, but the terrific wind continually threatened to carry the fire across, now at one point, now at another. Moreover, some barn manure had been spread on this plow land, and this, taking fire and blowing everywhere in the terrific wind, made our situation quite desperate for a while. However, we at last won to the extent of saving the buildings. This fire, together with the one which raged next day, when the wind was still more terrific, did enormous damage, burning out, in part or whole, even some of the older settlers, such as James Hoxeng and others. The town of Volin was almost completely destroyed. Some who had suffered loss in the previous fire were again burned out in part or whole, and the grass, as was the case after such a fire, was damaged for years to come. Many are the stories of narrow escapes in saving their homes and even their lives told by the old timers in connection with these fires. Sometimes there would be a whole company of women and children out on the middle of a plowed field, having fled there as the only refuge.

In every new country the Fire King, as tho endowed with a dramatic instinct, seems to end his performances with a grand climax. So here this was the last prairie fire of any consequence in that part of the country. King Corn from now on began to reign and the Fire King had to abdicate his immemorial sway and boundless dominions.

Chapter XIV
The Great Blizzard Of 1888

Even at the risk of seeming to chronicle too many of the hardships and afflictions of those times, I feel that I cannot leave this decade of our pioneer life without referring to the great blizzard of Jan. 12th, '88, for that, too, is a landmark and one which brings sad memories to many a South Dakotan of those years. The writer was merely a young boy then, yet the experience of that storm is very vivid in my mind.

The day opened bright and very mild, almost thawing, with no premonition that it held in store untold suffering, terror and death to man and beast, such as no other day has held for South Dakota. There was considerable loose snow on the ground, but the day being exceptionally pleasant up till noon and after, men were out on their various errands of going to town, hauling hay or other out-door occupations. The cattle, too, taking advantage of the mild day, were in the corn stalks and generally had scattered out some distance from the buildings. It being shortly after noon when the storm struck, many cattle were being taken to water, which in those days was often a considerable distance from the stables.

Suddenly and without the slightest warning, upon this peaceful unsuspecting scene, the storm burst forth in all its deadly fury. The wind having suddenly whipped around to the northwest, the temperature fell in a very short time as much as 60 and 70 degrees. The wind coming at the rate of about 60 miles an hour, picked up the loose snow and whipped it into a fine powder, rushed over the prairie as it were a rapidly moving wall of snow and fine particles of ice. Thus the air was so thick with fine snow, driven along by the furious storm, that it became very difficult to breathe and almost impossible to open one's eyes even for a moment. This choking, blinding effect of the storm soon exhausted either man or beast and, of course, all sense of direction was lost. Thus it seems probable that many of the victims were at first choked into exhaustion before they froze to death.

Many narrow escapes are told of that day. But there were also many who narrowly missed finding a shelter and never lived to tell their experiences. Some lost their way even between house and barn, and some were found frozen only a few rods from the house they had tried to find, but in vain. This was the case with two girls to the east of our place, who in going out to look for a younger brother never came back but were found frozen to death a short distance from the house. My younger brother Sivert and I were at the barn when the storm struck. We did the best we knew how for the cattle, Father being absent at a neighbor's and then we started for the house. We were only a short distance from the house and there was also a small building between, but even then we had to pause before starting out and take definite aim from where we were and then run, as we say, "for dear life". We reached the house to the great relief of Mother, who had become very anxious about us by that time.

The storm raged with merciless and demon-like destructiveness all that afternoon and all thru that night, with the temperature getting colder as the hours slowly rolled by. What terror and suffering the hours of that afternoon and fearful night brought to many, no one will ever know. There were those out in the storm, fighting desperately hour by hour with death, and in most cases only to find themselves rapidly nearing complete exhaustion. Then came the gradual numbness of all the sensibilities, followed by nature's merciful growing unconsciousness as drowsiness and sleep crept upon them and they at last stumbled over in the snow not to rise again. But tho the many tragedies and sufferings out in the open prairie that dreadful night were beyond words or imagination, yet scarcely less was the suffering of fathers, mothers and relatives of the lost ones who were utterly helpless in most cases even to attempt a rescue. These latter, as they listened to the merciless storm all thru that night, almost had a taste of the agonies of the lost world—if such a thing can be in this world. For in many cases their waiting thru the night was utterly without hope. If they knew their loved ones were caught by the storm some distance from the house, they also knew that there could be no hope. So they could only follow them in thought and imagination out there in the storm and the darkness as they were fighting their unequal and losing fight with the cruel, relentless storm. But even those who were in uncertainty as to the exact whereabouts of members of their families, like parents who had children in school, scarcely suffered less, for they had no assurance but that theirs, too, might be out there in the storm, and in many cases their worst fears proved to be the fact.

However, as all things come to an end, so this night of nights. The storm let up somewhat toward morning, and the new day at last came on, gray and terribly cold. The snow everywhere as far as eye could see lay piled up in great drifts. The prairie, especially near farm houses, was in many places dotted with frozen cattle, and other cattle still alive. There were over the country thousands and thousands of these cattle either already dead,

But let it not be inferred that we boys, and the girls, too, had no good times during those long summer days. The sun shone anyway most of the time, and we made the most of our opportunities while the sun shone. We boys hunted gophers, digging them out or drowning them out if near a pond; we dug Indian turnips in the spring and picked grapes, plums and berries in their season if we could get to them; built stone houses or caves; waded or swam in the sloughs or creeks; fished; fought snakes and skunks and sometimes one another. We traded jack knives, which were our chief valuables and consequently a standard medium of exchange; we braided long, long whips made from old boot legs or even willow bark; we broke young steers to ride on, at least attempted to, and sometimes they in turn nearly broke our necks by bucking and throwing us off; we concocted special modes of terrible punishment for exasperatingly troublesome members of our flocks. Much of the time, however, we could not get together or, as we said, "herd together". Then time passed more slowly and we had lots of time to think and even to brood over our job, which we considered about the worst there was in the world. However, with all its drudgery and sometimes loneliness and hardship, our job was a good preparation for the jobs that lay ahead of us.

Chapter XVI
Religious Movements And Workers Among These People

We have mentioned Reverends Nesse, Graven and Eielsen as pioneers in laying the foundations for the Church in these settlements. Among those who gave many years of service in the formative period of church development should also be mentioned Rev. Carlson, who followed Graven, who wrought for many years and at last found his resting place near one of the churches he had so long served. We cannot refrain from offering, altho a far too inadequate tribute, to one who has given the years of her life for the brightening and bettering of the lives of others; one who, altho not a pastor, yet as one pastor's devoted daughter and equally devoted as the wife of a succeeding pastor, gave the years of her young womanhood as well as the maturer years of her life to the service of these people—Mrs. C.T. Olberg, nee Carlson. For many years as a teacher in the parochial schools and continuously as a worker in the various activities of the church, especially among the younger people, and later as the pastor's wife, going in and out among the people, she has exerted an ennobling, Christianizing influence which only the angels of God and the far-off shores of eternity can estimate or measure.

There are many more, both men and women, lay-men and clergy, who have labored for their Master in this region, whose names I shall not be able to dwell upon, but whose names and records are in the Book of Life in Heaven and also written deep in the book of human life touched by them here on earth. Just to name two or three, there was Rev. Dahl of Gayville, who has put in a lifetime there. Then among the many visiting clergymen were Rev. G. Norbeck, Governor Norbeck's father, and a goodly number of others, lay and clerical preachers.

There were in the earlier years extensive "revivals", generally promoted by outsiders, often of other denominations, such as these of the middle eighties and middle nineties. There were other movements by laymen, both Lutheran and of other denominations. There were bitter controversies at times between the leaders of these movements, especially those promoted by men of other denominations than the Lutheran and the more strict adherents of the local churches. There were also bitter doctrinal controversies between members or adherents of the various branches of the Lutheran faith. Of the words said and the things sometimes done on these occasions none of the participants would be proud now, and I shall not perpetuate them by repeating what ought to be forgotten. The word "scorpion" is not just the right substitute for "Christian brother", but I distinctly recall that it was thus employed even between Lutherans.

Suffice it to say, there was often narrowness and intolerance on both sides, both as between denominations and between branches of the Lutheran Church itself. There was some good in most of these revival efforts and there were also some features which could justly be criticised.

There could be no doubt as to the sincerity of most of these revivalists, but being for the most part men and women of very limited education, they sometimes lacked balance and developed some vagaries. There were those who specialized on "Tongues" and on written revelations performed under spiritual ecstasy. Some had "revelations" that they should go to Africa to convert the heathen and a few actually went, soon returning sobered and saddened in their disappointment that the tongue gift did not enable them to understand, or to be understood by the natives.

Others advocated communism, baptism by immersion as indispensable to salvation, etc. In general there was a strong prejudice against any kind of church organization and to any regularly paid ministry. These extreme tendencies were, of course, a natural reaction against the evil in churches where a mechanical organization and the repetition of dead forms were all that reminded of what should have been a living spirit.

But to some people then and even now, a religious effort was either of God or of the devil, and consequently either wholly black or wholly white.

Then, too, when people believe, as many did and do still, that one's immortal salvation depends more on his holding a correct intellectual creed than on the spirit and fruits manifest in his life, it was inevitable that discussions of mere points of doctrine or creed, should become so intense at times as to lose wholly, for the time being, the Christian spirit. However, we shall, in this connection, give our pioneer fathers and first settlers credit for one great quality: They had convictions; they knew what they believed and believed it heart and soul. They did not, as some of this generation seem to do, doubt their beliefs and half believe their doubts.

In closing this brief outline of the religious activities of these people, allow me to give a boy's pleasant remembrance and loving tribute to one of the many traveling lay preachers who came to our house and also held services around in the neighborhood. John Aalbu and his good wife had settled near Ash Creek, Union county, in the sixties, and having retired from active farming in the eighties, they would drive the distance of 30-40 miles to our settlement on Turkey Creek several times a year. We children were always glad to see them. They had a top buggy, which in itself was of interest to us, as there was as yet no such luxury in our neighborhood. In this buggy, among other things, was always to be found a good sized tin can of smoking tobacco, for John and his wife both smoked. This was not considered as anything peculiar then or as objectionable on the part of the preacher and his wife, as it might be now. Now it seems that only women in the highest society may smoke. So amid clouds of the burning incense they would talk theology, religion, and also give practical hints on household and farm matters to their hosts, who were "newcomers." Mrs. Aalbu was a woman of very good mind and keen intellect. She would often correct a quotation from the Bible when not quite exact and serve as mentor to her husband when he, in the course of the service or some ritual, would forget something. It was only in later years, however, that he became ordained and in going thru the rituals at the various sacraments and services she was the "better half" in fact as well as name. This was owing to her splendid memory as also to her generally keen mind.

We did not see many strangers in those days, and how much these visits meant to us children as well as our parents! The discussions of fine theological points were often complicated and lasted far into the night, but we enjoyed them as well as we enjoyed our visitors. May God bless them, their work and their memory!

As an illustration of the subtlety of these discussions we might give a few of the topics: "Which Precedes in Christian Experience, Repentance or Faith?" "Faith or Works, Order of Precedence and Relative Worth." "Can a Man of His Own Accord and Strength Repent?" "Can a Christian in This Life be Wholly Sanctified?" "Free Will or Predestination?"

Chapter XVII
Biographical And Autobiographical Sketches

It has seemed best to include as a supplement to this narrative a number of sketches of individuals. Some of these individuals are already mentioned in the general narrative, and in such instances these separate narratives continue the record where we left off. Then there are some not mentioned in the general record but who belong by every right of circumstance to this Norse immigrant group and whose separate chronicles are of special interest and importance in view of our general purpose. This purpose, as already stated, is to hand down to the sons and daughters of the Norse pioneer immigrants a picture of the men and women who faced primitive nature in this part of the new continent and tamed it, causing the wilderness to bloom into the present prosperous, beautiful land.

A Daughter Settlement

(Narrated in part by H.B. Reese)

It was a winter day of 1902 that Father said to me, "I have had a letter from Halvor Hevle today. He wants to sell his land," he added. "Yes, I suppose he will have no use for that now, seeing he has moved away", I replied, and dismissed the matter from my mind. After a pause, Father said, "I thought you might buy it." I smiled at what seemed an absurd suggestion, for I had about a quarter of a dollar of money about me just then and no immediate outlook for ready money. I also knew that Father had none to lend me. So I replied: "He will have to sell his farm without money and without pay if I am to buy it."

Father thought for some time and finally added: "Hevle asks $1,000.00 for his land (¼ Sec.) and half of it cash. You can get a loan of $500.00 on it and he will be willing to take a second mortgage on the land for the balance."

Thus having nothing to risk in the deal, and moreover the idea of owning a farm of my very own kindling my ambition and appealing to my imagination, I readily agreed and the deal was made.

There was a fairly good dug-out on the place built up of stone and with a sod roof and board floor. The stable was of the usual kind, straw, with a little framework of rails and posts to support the roof and walls. But the layout seemed good to me because it was my own and the first home founded by myself.

I bought a team and broke some ground that summer, living at the old homestead one mile south. The next spring, however, I married a wife who consented to share the humble dwelling with me, and it became my home. Her maiden name was Hanna Bjorlo.

Soon, however, I was given to realize that in going into debt and in founding a home of my own I had assumed new responsibilities and burdens hitherto unknown. Thus after going into debt not only for the land but for the necessary equipment to work it and a few household necessities, we entered upon the year 1904 of notorious crop failures. It was also the time of a great financial depression. So that fall, instead of the original debt of $1,000.00, I found myself involved to the extent of $1,700.00 with little to show for it besides putting in two years of hard toil.

In this situation of seeming failure I began to think that farming of all occupations rewarded its devotees most stingily. A fellow gives to it the best of his years and strength and moreover allows himself to be tied down to a place only to be rewarded with crop failures and ever increasing accumulations of debt.

However, when one has the responsibilities of a family one cannot well run away from a situation no matter how bad, even if one were inclined to do so, the only possible procedure seemed to be to appease ones creditors as far as possible, get an extension of time and try again. I sold 40 acres of my farm, being the only thing I could sell, for $450.00. This tided us over until the next year when we hoped for better fortunes.

The next year came and brought us a better crop, but the prices were most discouraging. In 1895-6 I sold wheat at 43-45c per bushel, flax for 48c, corn 15-18c and oats 13c. Hogs were from $2.50 to $2.80 per cwt; cattle were from $15.00 to $18.00 for a milch cow and $25.00 for a three-year-old steer. These prices continued more or less for several years. Hired help was, however, correspondingly low, being from $15.00 to $18.00 per month during the summer months.

Nevertheless, after nine years of toil on this place with varying fortunes, I was at last able to pay for the place and also to make considerable improvements in buildings, both for the family and my accumulation of stock. The place, in fact, was beginning to look quite homelike, with trees and more sightly and comfortable buildings as well.

One would now expect me to feel somewhat satisfied and gradually settled down there for the rest of my days, raising our family and enjoying what we had or came to have. We had a nice little farm three miles from town with our old friends, neighbors and near relatives all around us.

There is a trait in human nature which is designated by various names according to the individual point of view. Some call it ambition, or forward looking; others, greed, covetousness, etc. The underlying idea seems to be a sort of discontent with one's present conditions and attainments, no matter what they are, a sort of forever reaching out for something greater ahead; to expand, explore new paths and to risk in the hope of winning. Whether this trait is good or otherwise, I shall not attempt to discuss, but I do know that it is strong in most of us and often dominating.

Thus I happened to make a trip to Charles Mix county (Bloomington) in 1902. The land there was much more level and the country more open than where we lived in Yankton county. So it looked to me to have more advantages for farming on a large scale. Moreover, the land was cheaper than where we were. So before returning home I had bought a quarter section near Bloomington, and that next spring we moved unto a rented place adjoining it.

But we had not been there a year before I realized my mistake. The level land did not produce the crop which we had anticipated, and there was not nearly the chance for cheap pasture either that we had been led to believe. Any free range was a thing of the past. We had a good start in cattle now, and I began to look around for some place in the northwest where there would be more room and more chance for this enterprise.

To understand my next move it is necessary to go back in our family tree to another branch and its development.

My brother, J.B. Reese, who had gone away to college about the time I began my independent farming, had now entered the work of the ministry and had been called to Wessington Springs and to care for the church work in the surrounding country as well. On a visit home he had told us of the cheap land and the fine opportunities in that new country, especially for cattle. A little later he bought a section of land up there, getting his brother S.B. and sister, now Mrs. Nysether, and also Martin Nysether to each take one quarter with him. The land was bought for $5.00 per acre, and as far as the three last named owners were concerned "sight unseen".

As an illustration of how seemingly small circumstances lead to great issues in our lives, I recall the first trip I made to size up this section of land which I contemplated buying for the parties above mentioned and myself. It was the year after the last big fire, the notorious one of 1899, I believe. The fire had seemingly burned the very roots out of the ground, so that the little grass visible at the time of our visit in the latter part of July, was in tufts here and there with vacant spaces in between. As I stood on the hill, east of the present buildings on the J.B. Reese place, the land looked so poor and desolate that I almost lost "my nerve" as far as recommending it to my partners for purchase, even with all the faith I had in the new country generally. But as I stood there realizing that the whole decision rested with me whether to buy or not, I noticed an angling trail across the corner of the land to the northeast along which the fire had been put out. But the thing which drew my interest particularly was that on the other side of this trail, or where the fire had not gone the grass was much better. This decided me. I purchased the land mostly on credit. This led to my brother's coming up and buying and finally moving up. His coming in turn led to the coming of practically the whole present settlement.—Editor.

In August 1902 a friend by name of Ole Sletten and myself started out to drive overland to see this country of which we had already heard interesting reports thru my brother. We spent the first night of our journey at Bridgewater, and the country around there seemed good to my partner. But when we reached Mitchell and vicinity, where the soil was sandy and dry, so that the prairie was quite seared over, it being in the month of August, my partner thought we might as well turn back, as there would be no use in exploring farther into a country like that. The grass was too short and scant. Moreover, the buildings and other improvements along the way gave no suggestion of prosperity among the farmers. Up thru Hutchinson county we passed a great many of the long, low mud houses belonging to the Russian German settlers there. These, too, were responsible for our poor impression of the northwest country at this point.

Nevertheless, we proceeded to Wessington Springs, where we met my brother, J.B. Reese, who took us out the next day to see the land he had bought and the country generally. We went out some 15-16 miles southwest of Wessington Springs, and if the land had seemed poor to us before, now it seemed only worse. We passed a considerable number of empty houses which indicated that the inhabitants had been forced to abandon the land on which these stood. It was in August and dry so that the prairie was quite seared over. Then, too, the last big prairie fire which ravaged this section had just gone thru a couple of years before, destroying the greater number of the buildings on the many abandoned homesteads and also burning the very roots out of the ground. What grass was left, or rather roots, stood in tufts with a big vacant space of ground between these tufts.

My partner did not express himself much as to the new country, but what he thought about it can be guessed by the fact that he wanted none of it for his own. However, I bought a quarter section of it adjoining the tract which J.B. Reese had already bought, before returning home, thinking it might do for pasture. I paid less than $5.00 per acre for it, so I felt that I could not lose much anyway.

May we digress for a moment here and point out the history of the original homesteaders of this section we are just describing, for it is full of interest and has also not a few of the tragedies of the prairie. This part of the state has seen more than the average of the disappointments incident to pioneer life. It has been the grave-yard of many bright hopes and furnished a burial place instead of a building place for not a few pioneers of the prairie.

The valley between Templeton to the north and Crow Lake to the south, with some of the adjacent land as well, was settled mostly by people from New York, Virginia and Pennsylvania in the early eighties. These people had some means, according to the standards of those times; were above the average pioneer in education and in general started in to build homes embodying not merely necessary shelter but even refinement and comforts. They planted trees, both shade and fruit trees; also flowers and shrubs.

The first years of their settlement were sufficiently wet and the crops were correspondingly good, some getting upward of 30 bushels of wheat per acre on the newly broken ground. This encouraged the settlers even to going into considerable debt for equipment to carry on larger farm operations. Land rose in value from free homesteads to $300.00 to $500.00 per quarter. Then came the dry years of 1893-'4-'5 and others as well of small or no crops. Not only no crop, but all the wells dried up so there was the greatest scarcity of water for man and beast. Many of these people were heavily in debt and it was almost impossible to borrow any more to tide over the emergency.

Then it was that the people began to stampede, as it were, going out as many as 30-40 in one company. Some who had many obligations but few scruples are said to have made their departure less conspicuously, quietly creeping away between sunset and dawn and without bidding anyone good-bye.

It was these conditions of the early years and the people who ran away from here to report their experiences far and wide which gave South Dakota a black eye and a bad name for years to come.

Yet after the great exodus, when the country was almost depopulated in a few months, there were found a few left behind. These were generally the ones who had had little or nothing to begin with and who now did not have enough to go anywhere else even if they wanted to do so. Those who were left by 1900 had gotten their second wind, as it were, having learned to adapt themselves to the country and were getting a start in cattle.

The big fire referred to above, sweeping over the section in '99 and destroying many of the vacated buildings, as also the remnants of orchards and groves, completed the wiping out of the visible monuments of the first settlers, so the country was nearly back again to the primitive conditions in the early years of 1900.

It was at this time (1904) that we decided to remove from Charles Mix county to Jerauld and the vicinity just described. To move such a distance overland with all one's belongings, including cattle, as also a family in which were several small children, and in the treacherous month of March, was no joy ride for any one concerned. After looking about for a partner in this difficult enterprise, I finally made arrangements with one, Knut Lien, to join me. He had about 40 head of cattle and was a single man. I took with me about 60 head, so on a morning in the early spring of 1904 my partner and I started with our first loads for the land of wide and roomy pasture if not of still waters. On the evening of the second day we stopped in front of the old house on my brother's place, which was to be our future home. But the situation which met us was not especially encouraging to tired, cold and hungry men. The window lights were broken; the floor, too, the house having been used for a granary, had given way. There was no shelter for our horses and, worst of all, not a drop of water on the place.

I was, indeed, discouraged at the outlook and said to Knut: "We will not unload. We shall rest until morning and then return." He made no reply, and after doing what we could for our horses we lay down on the floor to get what rest we could.

However, the next day the sun shone, and with the sunshine came renewed courage. We put some supports under the floor and unloaded our goods into the house. Then we went on to the springs for lumber and soon had a shed built to shelter the horses. But the lack of water was the worst of our needs and could not quickly be met. An artesian well had been put down the year before in anticipation of our moving, but it did not furnish any water even with a pump and wind mill. The shallow wells on the place, too, were dry. It became evident to us why the people who had preceded us in these parts had left the country.

However, having severed our connections where we had been living, and with our cattle to dispose of somehow, there seemed nothing to do but to go forward. So I returned to Bloomington, and hiring a man to help us, we started, now with all our belongings, for the new home. On the evening of the third day, or April 17th, 1904, we reached Crow Lake. We, ourselves, as well as the cattle, were very tired, so we camped there for the night, the family having gone on previously to the house we were to move into.

That night a snow and sleet storm broke upon us, lasting all of the next day. With no hay and worn out from the trip, the cattle began to succumb. Two were left on the place, nine died during the five or six miles which remained of the way, and still five more after arriving at our destination. Those which survived were so exhausted that it took them most of that summer to recover.

This, then, was our first taste of the new land, and it seemed at the time just a little bitter. My cattle dead or nearly so; nothing to do with; everything to be done.

However, during that spring we managed to get a new well sunk, 1260 feet deep, costing $650.00. I also put in 15 acres of wheat and 18 of barley with 90 acres of corn. Fortunately we got a good crop that year, which we also greatly needed.

At first it seemed rather isolated in those days. There were sometimes a couple of weeks in which we did not see a human being outside of our own family. The distance to Mr. Smith, our nearest neighbor to the north, was three miles. To the south, four miles, were Will Hughes and Will Horsten and also the Rendels. Then there was Mr. Gaffin and two or three others southwest of his place. So there was room and to spare between neighbors in those days and for some time following.

From this small beginning has now grown up a fine neighborhood with a good community church and congregation; rural mail delivery; phones; modern homes, and good roads. Among those who have helped build this splendid community should be mentioned besides those above, the Moen families, the Aalbus; the Fagerhaugs—Iver and Arnt; the Stolen brothers—Emericht, Olalf, and Martin; Vognild brothers; Bjorlos; Bjerkagers; Petersons, and others. It is a matter of just pride that out of this little group above mentioned, no less than seven young men served in the Great War. These were Reuben Peterson, Martin Peterson, Hugo Peterson, Ole Sneve, Martin Stolen, William Linsted, and Roy Goffin. Two of these—Reuben Peterson and Ole Sneve—were at the "front" for months and went thru some of the bloodiest battles of the War.—*Editor.*

Chapter XVIII
Looking Down The Trail To The Years Ahead

We have followed the trail of the first immigrants for more than half a century, from the time they left the old home until they have become an integral part of the life of the new home of their adoption. So marvelous has this experience been that to many it must seem almost like a dream or fairy tale. They came out of a land of poverty and hampering restrictions, social, political and religious. They found an opportunity to attain a comfortable living and a chance to help at the big job of working out a democracy. They came strangers to a strange land, they have already come to share in every position of trust and honor in the new land, with the exception of the presidency, including a number of governors. They came out a comparatively small company; they have become a multitude, there being already in this country more people of Norse extraction than the whole population of the mother country.

As we look around us among the particular groups here described, and see that the fourth generation from the pioneers is already coming on, the thought comes to us: "What of these people and their descendants a hundred years from now?"

As I, in vision and imagination, put my ears to the ground of present prophetic facts and tendencies, I hear the distant tramp of great multitudes out of the oncoming generations. Who are these multitudes which no man can number? They are the sons and daughters of the immigrant, tho outwardly indistinguishable from the Mayflower product which, too, are the descendants of immigrants. But while the Norse or Scandinavian immigrant is more quickly amalgamated in the sense of taking on all the outward colorings of his new environment than any other nationality, what, if any, will be his distinctive impress upon, or contribution to, the life he has come to share?

As there has been, and is, much foolish talk, malicious misrepresentation and manufactured-to-order hysterics about the "menace of the immigrant", on the part of pink-tea patriots and that whole breed of parasites who feed and fatten on stirring up and keeping alive class prejudice and hatred, I want to turn on the light here and now, the light of truth and facts.

In the first place, then, I wish to call the attention of these self constituted, Simon-pure and, in their own estimation, only Americans, to the fact that there is not in itself any disparagement to a man to be an immigrant or descendant of one. Did they ever read about the Pilgrim Fathers, George Washington, Ben Franklin or Abraham Lincoln? Well, these and multitudes of others they might read about were all "immigrants" or descendants of immigrants; not only that, but our self-appointed detractor of the immigrant is the descendant of immigrants—unless he or she is an Indian—and even the Indians are immigrants only of an earlier date.

In the second place, while the immigrant should ever be mindful, and in most cases is, of what the new land has offered him in opportunity, yet be it remembered also that, as far as the "natives" around him are concerned, he has given them immeasurably more than they have given him. He has done the great bulk of the rough, hard work of the mine, forest, factory and of subduing the untamed soil, and without him there would have been far fewer soft-handed jobs for his critics and far fewer of the comforts of life and developments of the country for all the people to enjoy. He has built the railroads, literally by the sweat of his brow, while the superior "native" manipulated them, watered their stocks and rode on them, finding that part of the enterprise more comfortable and profitable. But unless the "foreigner" had been willing to wield the shovel and lay the rails as well as roll them out red hot in the mill, where would the "American" have had a chance to shine in the deal?

Again, we are told that the immigrant comes here ignorant and without ideals and standards of life which would make him a safe member of a democracy. Of course, like most broad generalizations, this has a grain of truth when applied to some of the present influx from southern Europe. But when applied to immigrants generally, and especially to the class we have here described, the above judgment is just about the exact opposite of the truth. The illiteracy of the Norse immigrant is far less than that of the land of his adoption, in fact, practically negligible, and far less than that of any other class of immigrants. As for ideals of life and standards of morality, the immigrant was generally deeply shocked, on arriving here, at the lawlessness, profanity, sordidness, crass materialism and godlessness prevalent among the people around him who called themselves Americans.

And speaking of "ideals" he came here in most instances because of his ideals of freedom—religious, political and economic; to have a chance to live out and express these ideals. They built schools and churches while many of them themselves lived in sod houses or dugouts. Their sons and daughters are found in every college and university of the Northwest and out of all proportion to their rank in the total population. They more than take their share in the four learned professions of teaching, medicine, the ministry and the law. In other words, he came for the very same reason that the first immigrants, or Pilgrim Fathers came—to find room for his growing ideals, as already shown in this narrative. Then, of course, like them, he also came to better himself economically thru realizing certain ideals of equality of opportunity which he had come to cherish in his home land.

Some time ago, Sinclair Lewis, the noted author, speaking on this subject, said:

"I chose 'Carl Erikson' as the hero, protagonist, whatever you call him, of the 'Trail of the Hawk' because he is a typical young American. Your second or third generation Scandinavian is the best type of American. *** They are the New Yankees, these Scandinavians of Minnesota, Wisconsin and the Dakotas. They have mastered politics and vote for honesty, rather than handshakes. **** They send their children thru school. They accumulate land, one section, two sections, or move into town and become Methodists and Congregationalists, and are neighborly. *** And in a generation, thanks to our flag-decked public schools, they are overwhelmingly American in tradition."

"Boston, Dec. 16. President Charles W. Elliot, who in an address before the Economic Club of this city has declared in favor of an unrestricted immigration and proclaimed the ability of this country to 'digest' the newcomers of every religion, education and nationality, has been at the head of Harvard University since 1869, was a graduate of that institution in the class of 1853, and holds the degree of LL.D. from Williams, Princeton and Yale. He is considered one of the highest living authorities in his specialty of chemistry and has written many scientific works."

Permit me to offer a word of caution in this connection regarding certain tendencies and attitudes toward the immigrant which are working just the opposite result from what is intended.

There is that splendid movement inaugurated during the war—the Americanization movement. Many, and I would like to believe most of the workers in this movement, approach the recent immigrant with understanding and respect and not with that disgusting provincial type of mind and patronizing air which we see here and there. Now it should be said very emphatically that any one who regards himself as a superior being merely because born on this side of the Atlantic and the immigrant as an inferior because born on the other side, should keep his or her hands off Americanization if for no other reason, for this one: They are not themselves in any true sense Americans, lacking both the American spirit and ideals. It is such sociological tinkerers that often de-Americanize more immigrants than the others can Americanize. These recent comers are as keen to detect a patriotic sham as any native, and their disgust and resentment of it is profound. And the inevitable result is that they will judge the country by its supposed representatives.

Even such organization as the American Legion and Home Guards should refrain from every appearance of functioning as spies and censors of the immigrant or even of organizations which may be considered radical so long as they do not clearly advocate lawlessness or violence. Yellow paint, personal violence and breaking up of peaceable assemblies, in short, lawlessness, such as has already taken place over the country, will not tend to teach regard for law or love for country on the part of the victims. A mother cannot gain the love of a child or even respect by the abuse of force, neither can a government or organization inculcate patriotism by petty persecution and abuse.

There are over one hundred ex-service men in this state who are the sons and grandsons even of the few pioneers described in this memorial. I had the privilege of addressing a part of them at the home coming last summer. Let me say to such of them as may read these pages: Do not permit selfseeking men, small Americans, to borrow your splendid organization and glorious prestige to carry out their petty aims or personal spites. Be such big Americans that more recent arrivals seeing you, cannot help but admire you and learn to love the country which could produce you. This is real Americanization.

Have these people then a peculiar racial contribution to make to the civilization of which they have become a part, and will they make it? As to the latter, all I can say is that we should all make it our sacred aim, privilege and duty to deliver this our gift. I am sure we have it.

What then is it? In the main it may be summarized in a few words: Industry, Thrift, a Sane Conservatism, Social Genuineness and Religious Devotion.

I cannot believe that any one who knows the Norse immigrant would deny that the above are outstanding expressions of his character and life. The "newcomer" was not perhaps very "smart" in the Yankee sense, and God forbid that he ever should become so, but he was a hard, persistent worker, and he *saved*. The man who lived "by his wits" or by hook and crook was not often found in his class, nor was he encouraged in his efforts if found.

In this age of enormous over-production of non-producers; of innumerable hordes of swivel chair folks, of middle men, "manipulators", runabouts, who are mostly parasites on the social organism, is there not need of emphasizing the production of something to meet real human needs?

There is much talk and theorizing about the cause or causes of the present high cost of living. There is, of course, no one single cause responsible for this situation so full of hardship for many and so great a menace to all. But one of the great causes, next to the shameless profiteering by middlemen, is the alarming over-production of non-producers. The great hordes of people who want somehow or other to live by the sweat of the other fellow's brow rather than their own; who by their clamor create innumerable jobs—paper jobs—in connection with national, state, and municipal government as also in connection with charitable and ecclesiastical organizations. It is a part of our mission as the sons of producers to say to these parasites: "You've got to get off the other fellow's back," at the same time calling him by his right name—industrial slacker, social pauper, bum.

So may we take for our slogan the great words of Carlyle: "Produce! In God's name, Produce!" Let us, like the Fathers, keep close to the world of real values and refuse to be enticed into that "paper world" which is one of the real menaces of our country, far more so than the "immigrant" ever was. In being industrious producers in our line, whatever it may be, we need not be "grinds". In being thrifty in an age of extravagance and criminal wastefulness, we do not need to be stingy or niggardly.

Yes, this our contribution is worth cherishing, for it is sorely needed today.

If industry and thrift are gifts which our fathers brought to this land and which we should hand on as our peculiar offering, no less is that of sane conservatism. In this age of social, economic, political and even religious wildcat schemes and propagandas, America needs a balance wheel. We need a sane conservatism that is not, on the one hand, the corpselike immobility of the typical stand-patters, or reactionaries to all progress, and who themselves are the cause of much insane radicalism. And, on the other hand, if true to our traditions and temperament, we shall not dance to everybody's fiddle without investigation of what sort of a tune is being played.

Ours, then, should be the open mind; the forward look, to examine, search out, weigh men and issues. When we, amid the hordes of voices who cry: "Lo here! Lo there!" occasionally find a prophet with a message, let us follow him. Let us be a "holy terror" to all cheap demagogs of every party and name, but let us also be the hope and support of every true prophet, political, industrial or religious. This is our part.

Social And Religious

There is a beautiful sincerity, a certain heartiness about our Norse friendships and social relationships which I have not found elsewhere. Writers in recent years have been bemoaning "the lost kindness" of the world. Among our immigrant people, at least, you will find the lingering fragrance of this old time kindness which for many in this age of pretense and social sham relations has become only a sad, sweet memory of the long ago. I charge us all, as inheritors and trustees of this precious treasure—social sincerity and genuine kindness—let us cherish it, cultivate it and guard it as one of the very greatest valuables of life. For what is life without this, even with all the fine houses and lands, automobiles and aeroplanes? On the other hand, what is life with this genuine spirit of brotherliness in it? With this you can have the lights of Heaven and music of the spheres in a sod shanty. For where real good will is, Heaven is near. So let this beautiful sincerity, or heartiness, vitalize your handshake, flame in your look and thrill in your word of greeting to the fellow traveler over life's way.

If our Norse immigrant has a distinctive contribution to make to America, industrially, politically and socially, no less certainly has he an offering to make to the highest and most important department of life, that of religion. The Scandinavian is almost instinctively religious. You find among them comparatively few specimens of that sleek, beefy, selfcomplacent, godless animal-type, so frequently encountered today in other quarters. The immigrant had encountered too many of the realities of life; had been too often face to face with the ultimate facts of life and existence, to develop the shallow conceits of a mere beef animal whose main experience of life has been largely confined to a full stomach and the animal comforts. Not strange that this creature should speak great swelling words against the Church, the Christ and His followers, as well as against God Himself. The fool has always said in his heart (and with his stomach): "There is no God".

Because of this deep religious devotion characteristic of the Norse immigrant, and evolved amid the majestic mountains, the thundering rivers and water falls, as well as the loudly resounding sea of his birthplace, he built altars to God and established his worship almost as soon as his feet touched the new soil. Partly because of his religious sincerity the expression of his religious life has sometimes showed a certain narrowness of outlook and an intolerance of different religious forms which has not been to his credit. It is because of this latter trait that so many of the Norse immigrants and their descendants have been driven from the church of their fathers and are found in almost every religious sect in the country. We have heard "infant damnation" in its rankest form preached within the last year, and other doctrines as well, which are remnants of Mediaeval barbarism and which most Lutherans today would repudiate. Yet we believe the God of Jesus Christ is becoming more clearly seen, and that the wider horizons of truth are appearing. However, this is my plea: May we cherish the religious devotion, the real piety characteristic of our forebears. This is a contribution greatly needed in an age of religious indifference, if not open hostility. And keeping alive in us and inculcating in our children this religious devotion, may we never be numbered among that class who religiously are lukewarm, neither hot nor cold, only fit to be spewed out of the mouth of God and man. Let us be a salt in the religious life of our country, for without genuine religion there can be no morality worth talking about among the mass of mankind; and without morality we can never succeed in developing, or even keeping from destruction, our experiment in democracy. So may we put this, too, our supreme gift, on the altar of our country.

Now we close our humble effort with a word of tribute to those brave, unselfish men and women who left home, friends and native land, that we, their children and descendants, may have a better chance at life and happiness. They have paid the price of those who have to take and to hold the front lines in the great struggle with untamed nature in a new, uninhabited country. Many are the premature graves, the lonely heartaches and tragedies, most of which only God knows. They have laid the material foundations for us deep and strong. They have also left us an inheritance of ideals and characteristics to hand on to the coming generations. If "American" is a state of mind, a certain kind and quality of ideals and aspirations, rather than a matter of birthplace, then our immigrant fathers and mothers were often more American than the native born. However, in any case these characteristics and ideals above enumerated are the life of our nation and ours to keep alive. And in holding aloft as our slogans, these ideals of industry, thrift, sane conservatism, genuineness and religious devotion, we shall both build the noblest possible monument to the immigrant and also lay the sure foundations for the great future before us and our children.

To the few men and women who still remain of the first generation of immigrants, let us show our love and respect while they still linger with us, for it will not be long that we can have the opportunity. When some political demagog, under the thin guise of super-patriotism, would by legislation or social odium deprive them of the consolations of religion in the old tongue to which they are accustomed, and thus send them with sorrow if not bitterness to their graves, let us have the courage and the manhood to fight these contemptible grand-standers openly and to a finish. The language question will solve itself in a few years in any case and without this violence and insult to a few lingering men and women who have served this country so well and who are now asking only that they be allowed to pass undisturbed to their grave. There they will rest from their labors, but their works will follow after them.